Fighting Corruption in Public Services

Fighting Corruption in Public Services

Chronicling Georgia's Reforms

THE WORLD BANK
Washington, D.C.

1 2 3 4 15 14 13 12

This volume is a product of the staff of The World Bank with external contributions. The findings, interpretations, and conclusions expressed in this volume do not necessarily reflect the views of The World Bank, its Board of Executive Directors, or the governments they represent.

The World Bank does not guarantee the accuracy of the data included in this work. The boundaries, colors, denominations, and other information shown on any map in this work do not imply any judgment on the part of The World Bank concerning the legal status of any territory or the endorsement or acceptance of such boundaries.

ISBN (paper): 978-0-8213-9475-5
ISBN (electronic): 978-0-8213-9476-2
DOI: 10.1596/978-0-8213-9475-5

Library of Congress Cataloging-in-Publication
Fighting corruption in public services: chronicling Georgia's reforms.
    p. cm. — (Directions in development)
  Includes bibliographical references.
  ISBN 978-0-8213-9475-5 (alk. paper) — ISBN 978-0-8213-9476-2
  1. Corruption—Georgia (Republic)—Prevention. 2. Organizational effectiveness—Georgia (Republic) 3. Municipal services—Government policy—Georgia (Republic) 4. Georgia (Republic)—Politics and government—21st century. I. World Bank.
  HV6771.G28F54 2012
  364.1'323094758—dc23

                                                                    2011052833

Cover photo: Giorgi Barsegyan, World Bank. Strolling through Shota Rustaveli Avenue, Tbilisi.
Cover design: Naylor Design, Inc.

Contents

Figures

Tables

Foreword

There is ample evidence that corruption holds back countries' economic development and erodes their citizens' quality of life. Millions of people around the world encounter administrative corruption in their daily interactions with public services, especially in developing countries. In many countries, administrative corruption imposes a heavy burden on citizens' and firms' time and resources, creates dissatisfaction with public services, undermines trust in public institutions, and stifles business growth and investment. Very often, it is the poor and the vulnerable who suffer the most.

Often, administrative corruption is seen as endemic, a product of traditional local culture, and—as such—inevitable. In turn, political leaders often use citizens' perceived tolerance of corruption as an excuse for inaction. Global experience is replete with stories of reform failures and dashed expectations, but relatively few successful anticorruption efforts. Georgia's experience shows that the vicious cycle of ostensibly endemic corruption *can* be broken, and—if sustained with appropriate institutional reforms—can be turned into a virtuous cycle.

This book, *Fighting Corruption in Public Services: Chronicling Georgia's Reforms*, is a story worth telling. It takes a case-study approach to *chronicle* how transparency and integrity in specific public services—traffic police, tax, customs, electricity distribution, higher education, issuance of identity documents, property and business registration, and municipal services—were improved. The book places particular emphasis on documenting the design and implementation of these reforms, attempting to shed light on the decision-making processes on reform design, the trade-offs policy makers faced, and the sequencing and complementarities among the various reforms. It does *not* seek to evaluate Georgia's approach to reducing corruption, but to identify the key political economy factors that contributed to the anticorruption reforms in Georgia. In particular, it highlights the critical importance of top-level political will, which enabled the prompt implementation of a strategy characterized by mutually reinforcing reforms for corruption prevention, detection, and enforcement in a wide range of public services. It also lays out the unfinished agenda of institutional reforms, which will be needed to ensure the sustainability of Georgia's anticorruption results by putting in place a robust system of checks and balances.

Not all of what Georgia has done may be replicable in other countries with different institutional and political economy contexts. Yet there are many useful lessons that could be adapted and applied in other countries facing comparable challenges in tackling pervasive administrative corruption.

Philippe H. Le Houerou
Vice President, Europe and Central Asia Region
The World Bank

Acknowledgments

This book would not have been possible without the strong support and valuable contributions of many people. Its authors would like to express their special gratitude to H.E. Mr. Mikheil Saakashvili, the president of Georgia; Mr. David Bakradze, speaker of the Parliament; Mr. Nika Gilauri, prime minister; and many others who contributed their time and effort for this book.

The book benefited from discussions with its advisory council, comprising Ms. Eka Gigauri, executive director, Transparency International, Georgia; Mr. Devi Khechinashvili, chairman of the board, Partnership for Social Initiatives (PSI); Mr. Lasha Bakradze, director of the Giorgi Leonidze State Museum of Georgian Literature; Mr. Akaki Gogichaishvili, editor-in-chief and presenter of "Business Courier" on Rustavi-2 TV channel; and Ms. Tamar Lebanidze, chair of the supervisory board, Bank Constanta, Georgia.

This book was prepared by a World Bank team led by Asad Alam and Van Roy Southworth and comprising Ekaterine Avaliani, Mariam Dolidze, Maia Duishvili, Ahmed Eiweida, Elene Imnadze, Tatyana Kandelaki, Nino Kutateladze, Joseph Melitauri, Inga Paichadze, and Stephanie Gruner (consultant). Luca Barbone, Michael Edwards, M. Willem van Eeghen, Faruk Khan, Andrew Kircher, Larisa Leshchenko, Thomas Lubeck, Kazi M. Matin,

Meskerem Mulatu, Pedro Rodriguez, Owen Smith, Tamara Sulukhia, and Yvonne Tsikata provided useful comments. Thanks are also due to the peer reviewers, Marcelo Giugale, Carlos Felipe Jaramillo, and Ritva S. Reinikka. This book would not have been possible without the inspiration and guidance of Philippe H. Le Houerou, vice president of the Europe and Central Asia Region of the World Bank.

About This Book

This book chronicles the anticorruption reforms that have transformed public service in Georgia since the Rose Revolution in late 2003. The focus is on the "how" behind successful reforms of selected public services. How did Georgia succeed when many other countries have failed, even after revolutions? How did the new government make reform happen? How can Georgia's success be replicated in other countries? How can Georgia's success be sustained? What is the unfinished agenda?

This book tries to answer some of these questions. It is based largely on data and informed by interviews with past and current high-ranking government officials who provide insights from within government on the challenges and solutions, the decisions, and the trade-offs considered.

This book does not assess Georgia's overall reforms since the Rose Revolution. It does not address efforts toward democratization, which were a key part of the Rose Revolution. The book focuses on how the state was able to root out corruption and eliminate red tape in selected public services. It does not analyze areas in which government efforts are still continuing or may have fallen short. Nor does it suggest any causality between anticorruption reforms and growth or social outcomes. The analysis and conclusions in this book are based on eight areas where anticorruption reforms have been successful: creating the patrol police, strengthening tax collections, cleaning up customs, ensuring reliable power supply, deregulating businesses, making public and civil registries work, rooting out corruption in university entrance examinations, and decentralizing municipal services. From the case studies on each of these efforts, the book identifies a set of common factors that led to the success of the reforms.

CHAPTER 1

Introduction

The atmosphere was tense and charged on the cold and cloudy night of November 22, 2003. Georgia's beleaguered and stoic population had finally had enough, with pervasive corruption, ever-present crime, and dysfunctional public services. Street demonstrations had grown in intensity every day since the flawed, corruption-riddled parliamentary elections several weeks earlier. While President Eduard Shevardnadze gave his inaugural address to the newly seated Parliament, the crowd seethed outside. When the demonstrators breached Parliament's door—many carrying roses, symbolizing the peaceful nature of the antigovernment demonstrations—they could not have known that they were about to usher in a period of unprecedented anticorruption reform.

In 2003, corruption permeated nearly every aspect of life in Georgia. Perhaps the most visible and hated manifestation of the pervasive corruption was the traffic police. Dressed in shabby Soviet-era uniforms, the mostly corpulent traffic police were stationed at nearly every road crossing in the country. They wielded wooden batons to flag down hapless motorists and extort bribes, usually for fabricated infractions. Motorists were not the only targets; the bribe-hungry traffic police often nabbed pedestrians as well.

Most other government services were also rife with corruption. Bribes were needed to get a passport, register property, start a business, or build a home. Entrance to state universities required bribes, and additional payments helped secure good grades and even degrees; mastery of subject matter was optional. Citizens paid officials to obtain driver's licenses (knowing how to drive was not required) and pass vehicle inspections. Restaurants bribed inspectors not to arbitrarily close enterprises that met sanitary standards and to turn a blind eye to enterprises that did not. Corruption in tax administration decimated revenue collection and spawned elaborate schemes to steal what little revenue was collected. Only a few people paid their utility bills, with many risking their lives to establish illegal power connections. Criminal gangs, called "thieves-in-law," operated with impunity, engaging in extortion, smuggling, carjacking, theft, and protection rackets. They often allied with government officials to rig contracts and otherwise plunder the treasury. Many corrupt government officials had been enriching themselves for years. State officials who officially earned $100 a month or less and were banned from holding a second job owned large villas and significant other assets, according to Zurab Adeishvili, the minister of justice. Prosecutors were also corrupt, routinely trumping up charges as a source of bribes with which to augment their salaries or finance legitimate investigations.

Early Reform Efforts: 1991–2003

Beginning in 1995—following a tumultuous period after independence that included three armed conflicts—the government restored some security and disbanded paramilitary groups that had vied for power since independence. It also made progress toward restoring macroeconomic stability. Georgia was ravaged not only by war and insecurity between 1992 and 1994 but also by hyperinflation and a collapsing economy. Inflation averaged nearly 7,000 percent over this period, and the economy contracted by more than 28 percent (table 1.1). Tax collection also collapsed, with public revenues falling from 15 percent of gross domestic product (GDP) in 1992 to 2.3 percent in 1993. The government stabilized the situation in 1995 by introducing a new currency, carefully managing the money supply, eliminating price controls, and reducing trade barriers. Nearly all key macroeconomic indicators improved significantly between 1992–94 and 1997 (table 1.1). After years of contraction, the economy grew at a rapid clip, inflation was tamed, and international reserves increased from about 3 weeks' to 2.5 months' worth of imports.

Table 1.1   Key Economic Indicators, 1992–2011

Indicator	1992–94	1995–97	1998–2003	2004–07	2008–11
GDP growth (percent)	−28.2	8.1	4.9	9.3	2.7
GDP per capita ($)	560	617	743	1,688	2,787
Inflation (average annual percentage change in consumer price index)	6,981.0	26.0	7.0	8.1	6.9
Government revenues (percent of GDP)	7.1	7.7	15.2	25.8	29.4
Government expenditure (percent of GDP)	37.5	15.7	18.8	27.6	35.2
International reserves (months of imports)	0.7	2.5	1.4	3.5	4.2
Poverty rate (percent of population below poverty line)	n.a.	n.a.	28.5	23.4	24.7

Source: World Bank staff calculations based on data from National Statistics Office of Georgia (GEOSTAT).
Note: Poverty is defined as monthly consumption of less than GEL 71.60 per person in 2007 prices.
GDP = gross domestic product. n.a. = Not available.

The recovery sputtered in 1998, as a result of the Russian crisis, drought, and the growing weight of government dysfunction in Georgia, though the macroeconomic situation, particularly with respect to inflation, remained stable. Growth between 1999 and 2003 averaged just under 5 percent a year, much of it coming from the one-time investment in the Baku-Tbilisi-Ceyhan oil pipeline. Rural areas suffered most from the collapse and benefited little from the listless recovery. Poverty in rural areas remained persistently higher than in urban areas. Revenue collection improved, particularly between 1995 and 1998, when it grew from about 5 percent of GDP to more than 14 percent, but growth in revenue stagnated thereafter through 2003.

Progress in other reform areas was spotty. Privatization of state enterprises was successful for small-scale enterprises and agriculture (60 percent of agricultural lands passed into private hands by the end of 1997). Little progress was made in privatizing large enterprises, however. One exception was electricity, where legislation was passed that set the stage for privatization and restructuring in the sector, including the privatization of the Tbilisi electricity utility.

The legal and regulatory framework for financial services was established. Reform of the judicial system also began. The centerpiece of this reform was the requalification of all judges based on objectively administered examinations. Judges who passed the qualification process were appointed for 10-year terms and given higher salaries and intensive training.

Early reforms in health care focused on privatizing services, sharpening the focus on primary care and prevention, and reducing the number of hospital beds and staff. Health outcomes improved modestly between 1995 and 2003 but did not recover to 1990 levels. (An exception was immunization rates, which rose dramatically.) The number of hospitals and staff was also reduced, albeit by less than targeted.

Education reforms began in 2001, focusing on a new curriculum, improved teaching methods and training, and greater autonomy for schools. Work also started on a national university entrance exam designed to eliminate corruption in university admissions.

Overall, the share of the budget going to the social sectors was small before 2003, and the little that was allocated was often sequestered because of shortfalls in revenue collection. Pension payments were 18 months in arrears by the end of 2003.

In 2000, the government launched an effort to tame the growing crisis of corruption in the public sector. President Shevardnadze appointed a group of seven experts to elaborate a national anticorruption program and guidelines for its implementation. In a radio address in March 2001, he pronounced that "the country's independence and its statehood, gained through the shedding of blood and tears, is on one pan of the scales, and corruption, with all its horrendous manifestations, is on the other." On the basis of the work of the expert group, the president signed two decrees in April and May 2001 authorizing the formation of a 12-member coordinating council and the creation of an anticorruption bureau. The council, chaired by the president himself, remained very active through November 2003. Several members of the council accused prominent government officials of corruption.

Despite the high profile of the council and the commitment of many of its members, little progress was made. The political will and capacity of the government to make changes simply did not exist. Nonetheless, these faltering first steps laid the foundation on which many of the reforms under the new government were built.

Emerging Reformers

Many reformers who took power in 2004 had gained valuable experience in President Shevardnadze's government before joining the opposition in frustration over the stymied reforms and continued corruption. President

Mikheil Saakashvili, who served as justice minister in the previous government, said of the old system, "It was like the old Soviet apparatus without central control from Moscow anymore. The good thing is that they allowed reformers to emerge, because there was loose control." Their experience in the old government gave several members of the new government insight into the inner workings of government and Parliament. They understood the entrenched system of corruption and had experimented with some initial efforts at anticorruption. In one of his last acts as justice minister, Saakashvili cemented his reputation as a corruption fighter when he disrupted a government meeting by displaying pictures of the mansions belonging to prominent government officials, alleging corruption and misuse of public funds.

Many of these reformers joined the opposition after leaving government, some as members of Parliament. The two main opposition parties, which coordinated to spearhead the demonstrations in November 2003, were the United National Movement, headed by Saakashvili, and the United Democrats, headed by Zurab Zhvania. The motto of the United National Movement was "Georgia without corruption." According to Minister of Justice Zurab Adeishvili, "We were always focused on corruption, because we understood that corruption was the major obstacle to the future development of Georgia." This focus on corruption resonated with the population. Popular support for the movement grew, leading to the protests that eventually culminated in the Rose Revolution and a new government committed to fighting corruption as a top priority.

Seizing the Opportunity

The government that was sworn into power in January 2004 was young, dynamic, and above all determined to help Georgia shed its legacy of post-Soviet collapse and despair. Its young reformers unleashed a program of reforms, unprecedented in its scope and ambition, that transformed Georgia within the span of a few years into an emerging middle-income, market-oriented economy.

The new government was armed with an overwhelming popular mandate. Saakashvili garnered more than 90 percent of the vote, and the United National Movement won about 68 percent of the seats in Parliament. From the outset, a small but strong team in the executive branch, united by a common vision and supported by a compliant Parliament and judiciary, drove the reform process.

The two most pressing problems facing the new government were a plundered treasury and a failed state, in which criminals and government officials were indistinguishable. Kakha Baindurashvili, a former minister of finance who worked closely with the late prime minister Zurab Zhvania, summed up the situation. "It was a disaster, it was not a state. The only way the previous government viewed the state was as a means to make money. All branches of government were corrupt." The first meeting of the cabinet revealed just how dire things were. The treasury was empty, and pension and salary arrears totaled more than GEL 400 million (almost $180 million). David Bakradze, who served in the National Security Council at the time and is currently the Speaker of the Parliament, recalled how bad the situation was. "I was participating in the first National Security Council Meeting the day after the revolution when the minister of defense stood up and said 'I don't have food for my soldiers, only enough bread left for a day and a half.' And then the minister of finance also stood and said, 'Well there is not a single tetri [cent] in the treasury now.'"

From this desperate beginning, the new government started its work, adopting a simple strategy. It sought to establish the credibility of the state from the outset by focusing on tax collection and the prosecution of criminals and corrupt officials. In one of his first acts, Zurab Nogaideli, the newly appointed finance minister, summoned tax collectors to a meeting at which they were told unequivocally that there would be zero tolerance for corruption and that henceforth they would be judged by their ability to collect revenue. At the same time, the government conducted high-profile arrests of renowned crime bosses as well as government officials and businesspeople suspected of corruption. As a result of these actions, money started pouring into government coffers, and every Georgian understood that the corruption that affected them daily would no longer be tolerated.

With money flowing into the treasury and an all-out assault on organized crime under way, the government turned to wiping out corruption and improving service in key public enterprises. The first priority was electricity supply. The government set a very ambitious target of restoring around-the-clock power throughout Georgia by the end of 2005. Achieving this target required both actions to stop corruption and improve bill collection and investments to rehabilitate a power system that was on the verge of total collapse.

At the same time, the government began parallel reforms in tax collection, public registries, business regulations, customs, traffic police, entrance exams for higher education, and municipal and local government. In each area the objectives were the same: to eliminate corruption and improve service. Although the objectives were common, reformers had considerable flexibility in the design and implementation of the reforms in their areas.

The Anticorruption Scorecard

Georgia achieved remarkable results in reducing corruption in a short period of time. Transparency International's Global Corruption Barometer ranked Georgia first in the world in 2010 in terms of the relative reduction in the level of corruption and second in the world in terms of the public's perception of the government's effectiveness in fighting corruption. In 2010, only 2 percent of Georgia's population reported paying a bribe over the previous 12 months.

Georgia also broke the connection between the state and organized crime. Crime rates fell sharply, to among the lowest in Europe, according to an international survey conducted by the Georgia Opinion Research Bureau International (GORBI) in 2011. In the 2012 *Doing Business* rankings, Georgia rose to 16th place—in the same group as many advanced countries in the Organisation for Economic Co-operation and Development (OECD). The successes led to what *The Economist* called a "mental revolution," exploding the widespread notion that corruption was a cultural phenomenon in Georgia (*The Economist* 2010).

By 2010, the prevalence of unofficial payments in various public services was very low (table 1.2). Most indicators were closer to those of the

Table 1.2 Prevalence of Unofficial Payments in Selected Public Services in Georgia and Comparator Groups of Countries, 2010

(percent of population surveyed)

Country/group of countries	Primary and secondary education	Road police	Official documents	Social security and unemployment benefits	Civil courts
Georgia	5	1	1	3	3
Former Soviet Union	23	30	20	17	20
New EU members	4	7	3	3	5
EU-5 (France, Germany, Italy, Sweden, United Kingdom)	1	0	1	1	1

Source: World Bank staff calculations based on data from World Bank and EBRD 2011.
Note: EU = European Union.

EU-5 than to the countries of the former Soviet Union or even the new member states of the European Union.

Progress in anticorruption in public services is evident across the board:

- The going "rate" to become a traffic cop was $2,000–$20,000 in bribes in 2003, depending on where the officer would be stationed. Since reform, hiring has been competitive and transparent. Overnight, 16,000 traffic police were fired, replaced a few months later with 2,300 new road patrollers. Staffing of all law enforcement agencies was reduced from about 63,000 in 2003 to 27,000 in 2011. Before the reforms, Georgia had 1 police officer for every 21 citizens; today, that ratio has fallen to 1 police officer for every 89 citizens. Police also now operate closer to the communities they serve.

- Georgians had no more than seven to eight hours of power a day in 2003—and in many parts of the country, only firms and families with influence and money received any power at all. Georgia now boasts 24-hour power supply and is a net exporter of power. Official collection rates of about 30 percent in 2003 meant that power utilities did not have the resources to manage their own finances; collection rates are now at 100 percent.

- Dealing with the state to set up a new business, or operate an existing one, was fraught with delays and corruption. In 2003, 909 permits and licenses were required, many of which could be bought and served no societal purpose. By 2011, the number of permits and licenses had been reduced to 137. Over 2003–11, the numbers of days needed to obtain a construction permit was cut from 195 to 98, and the number of procedures was reduced from 25 to 9. Through aggressive use of the "guillotine," reformers shut down entire government agencies that were not providing value and merely extracting bribes from the population.

- Corruption in municipal and local government was rampant before reform, and service delivery was shoddy. Over 2003–10, collection rates for water increased from 20 percent to 70 percent, and average daily water service rose from 4–6 hours to 16–18 hours. The water subsidy program was made more transparent by tying it to social assistance. The country's 1,110 local governments, whose large numbers and lack of accountability had facilitated corruption, were consolidated into just 69, and a system of elected mayors was introduced. Financing of local governments tripled, through a transparent equalization grant system and improved monitoring.

- In 2003, Georgia's tax base included just 80,000 taxpayers, and tax collections brought in just 12 percent of GDP. By 2010, the income tax base had increased to about 252,000 taxpayers, and collections represented 25 percent of GDP. These results were achieved through aggressive tax enforcement and major tax reforms, including the firing of corrupt officials, the competitive hiring of new staff, the elimination of arrears and nonpayments, the slashing of the number of taxes (from 22 to 5), the reduction in tax rates, the simplification of the tax code, and the rapid growth of e-filing of taxes, which accounted for almost 80 percent of all returns by 2011. Before reform, it cost about $5,000 to get a job at the lucrative Red Bridge crossing into Azerbaijan—an investment corrupt customs officials could quickly recoup through bribes. To reduce opportunities for corruption, the government cut the number of import tariffs from 16 to just 3. Firings and aggressive prosecutions of corrupt officials, competitive hiring of new staff, improved incentives and procedures, a new service culture, and automation all helped clean up the customs service.

- Informal payments were once the norm in public and civil registries. Introduction of a new culture, new staff, new technology, and new business processes has streamlined all interfaces between the citizen and the state—from registering a property to obtaining a passport—eliminating many opportunities for bribes.

- Bribes for university entrance were common before 2003, with university spots sold for $8,000–$50,000, depending on the department (admission to law school and medical school cost the most). The introduction of a common entrance exam and the institution of a transparent, competitive examination system eliminated corruption and improved access for many prospective students, especially the rural poor.

How Did the Government Do It?

The next eight chapters (chapters 2–9) present sector case studies of each of these areas of success. They describe the "how" of the anticorruption reforms, based on data and interviews with many of the key actors. Each chapter describes the corruption problem as of 2003, discusses the anti-corruption reforms adopted after 2003, and presents some of the results.

Strong accountability arrangements lie at the heart of the success of the reforms. These arrangements help ensure that the rules of the game are enforced and increase the sustainability of reforms. For each case study, the two-way interactions among the government, providers, and citizens/firms that underlie the success of the reform program are shown.

From these case studies, a set of 10 cross-cutting factors emerge that have driven Georgia's success story. These lessons can be summarized as follows:

1. *Exercise strong political will.* The overwhelming mandate from voters and the dire reality of the situation Georgia's new leaders inherited bolstered their will to act quickly and forcefully.
2. *Establish credibility early.* The new leaders struck hard against corruption to establish early credibility and extend the window of opportunity voters had given them. High-profile arrests of corrupt officials and criminals signaled zero tolerance for corruption. Early successes built support for further actions, in a virtuous cycle of reform.
3. *Launch a frontal assault.* Rather than spending precious time strategizing, worrying about sequencing, or consulting on action plans, the government launched a rapid and direct assault on corruption in a broad array of public services. It acted quickly to keep vested interests at bay.
4. *Attract new staff.* The leaders of the Rose Revolution formed the core of the government's executive branch. They looked outside politics and government to recruit qualified, often Western-educated, staff to spearhead the reforms and paid them well.
5. *Limit the role of the state.* The reformers shared a vision of limited government. They also believed that limiting contact between citizens and civil servants and slashing red tape reduced opportunities for corruption and was good for the economy.
6. *Adopt unconventional methods.* Extraordinary times required innovative approaches. A special fund financed from outside sources paid for increased salaries and bonuses for a short initial period. Jailed corrupt officials and tax cheats who admitted guilt and paid heavy fines were released from prison.
7. *Develop a unity of purpose, and coordinate closely.* A small group of policy makers, headed by the president, formed a core team that

shared common values, coordinated closely, and stayed together. Regular cabinet meetings and close ties with allies in Parliament facilitated coordination.

8. *Tailor international experience to local conditions.* The government borrowed from international experience in designing reforms, adapting foreign practices to local circumstances as needed.

9. *Harness technology.* The government used technology extensively to limit contact between the state and citizens, implementing e-filing of taxes, electronic payments for services, and traffic cameras.

10. *Use communications strategically.* Communication started at the top, with the president, whose message on corruption was clear and consistent. The media was key in investigating corruption and publicizing the sensational arrests of suspected criminals, tax cheats, and corrupt officials.

As the case studies bring out, what was unique about Georgia was strong political commitment, backed by the comprehensiveness, pace, boldness, and sequencing of the reforms and, most important, the strong role of the executive in implementing them. The last chapter of this book discusses these themes as well as the issues of sustainability and replicability to other countries.

The fight against corruption in public services is a universal and continuous one. The nature of the problems varies, and the solutions may differ, but the struggle continues in most societies. This book is about how Georgia made noticeable gains.

CHAPTER 2

Creating the Patrol Police

The State of Affairs in 2003

Corruption was at the core of Georgia's policing system. Police could not survive on the tiny salary they received—when they were paid at all (sometimes they went months without a paycheck). To make ends meet, many worked for organized crime or sold drugs or, as was common among traffic cops, accused citizens of breaking laws (whether they had or not) and then pocketed the fines.

People paid as much as $2,000–$20,000 in bribes for jobs as policemen, earning the money back through an internal pyramid scheme funded by illegal pursuits. Each week, for example, patrolmen paid a fixed amount from the bribes they extracted from citizens for various "offenses" to their immediate supervisors, who in turn were expected to share a cut with their bosses, and so on. Traffic cops were always on the take. On an hour's drive, one could expect to be stopped at least twice and asked to pay a small fine. Citizens had little choice but to pay up, whether they had broken laws or not. The corrupt system created a vicious cycle in which money rarely reached state coffers, salaries were not paid regularly, and police turned to crime to make money.

There was nothing secret about this. "Under the previous regime, government ministers would beg the finance minister for money to pay salaries. Only the internal affairs minister didn't bother. He'd say, 'Give me money for petrol and then my police will take care of their own salaries,'" says Speaker of the Parliament David Bakradze.

Police—particularly traffic police—were consistently rated among the most corrupt public officials in Georgia. A 2000 survey estimated that when stopped by traffic police, motorists were asked for bribes in 7 out of 10 contacts (GORBI 2000). Enterprises reported that when given the opportunity, the traffic police extracted bribes 31 percent of the time. According to the same survey, public officials, enterprises, and households alike ranked the honesty and integrity of traffic police among the lowest of any public official.

Distrust ran so deep that crimes went unreported. People were afraid to mention even minor infractions, such as unruly teenagers breaking windows, for fear that culprits would be tortured in detention. Their fears were not unfounded. A 2002 UN Human Rights Committee expressed concern about "widespread and continuing subjection of prisoners to torture and cruel, inhuman or degrading treatment or punishment by law enforcement officials and prison officers" (Civil.ge 2002).

Police were also considered hopeless at solving crimes. If someone's house was robbed, citizens typically turned to people linked to criminals to offer a ransom to get their belongings back. Worse, many police were themselves criminals, involved in kidnapping, drug dealing, and racketeering. Officials at the highest levels were tied to the criminal network of "thieves-in-law." This network was initially formed as a society for ruling the criminal underworld within Soviet prison camps. Over time, it evolved into a network of organized criminals acting in accordance with special rules and gaining profit through intimidation, threats, and crime. The high ranks in the law enforcement system reportedly had close ties with the thieves-in-law, protecting and conducting business with its elite.

Post–2003 Anticorruption Reforms

Nowhere did the government act more boldly than in its efforts to transform the traffic police—the very symbol of corruption in Georgia. Reform began by severing the ties between the government and organized criminals. It went on to create a whole new cadre of patrol police.

Severing the Ties between the Government and the Criminal World
For the thieves-in-law, implementation of the new policy was devastatingly quick: they were routed before they had a chance to organize

resistance. With television cameras rolling, truckloads of heavily armed police in ski masks rounded up high-profile crime bosses. There were no half-measures. If a person resisted arrest, he could be shot, according to an 2005 internal ministry decree; 21 criminal suspects and 16 police were killed in police operations in 2005 (24 Saati 2006).

The regime had changed, and word soon spread. New anti-mafia legislation was instrumental in crushing the thieves-in-law. The new criminal code and amendments, which borrowed heavily from the Italian anti-mafia model and the Racketeer Influenced and Corrupt Organizations (RICO) Act in the United States, were introduced in the first six months of 2004 (they underwent further revisions through 2009 to close loopholes). A New Zealand law on harassment and criminal association and a British conspiracy law designed to fight criminal groups also influenced the legislation. The new legislation enabled authorities to confiscate money and property of illicit origin and introduced the concept of plea bargaining.

A law on organized crime rackets was enacted at the end of 2005, aimed specifically at the thieves-in-law. In a unique feature, the legislation made it a crime to be a thief-in-law or a member of the "world of thieves" who followed the thieves' code of conduct. This addition was particularly effective because part of the code of conduct was that if asked, a member of the world of thieves could not deny being a member.

The government viewed its strong-handed approach toward establishing law and order as essential to making people think differently, destroying respect toward the criminal underworld, and demonstrating the authority of formal legal institutions over informal ones. Between 2006 and 2010, 180 members of the thieves' world were prosecuted and convicted; as of 2011, some 35 mafia leaders remained in jail. Many others fled the country. The state also confiscated about $1 billion worth of property from mafia bosses and corrupt state officials, according to Minister of Justice Zurab Adeishvili. Some of the confiscated houses became government offices; others became police stations.

Reforming the Traffic Police

Another challenge was to restore the credibility of the traffic police—a tall order, given that it had none. "Everyone agreed that the traffic police were the most visible sign of corruption, and so there was immediate consensus that it was an obvious thing to go after," explains Vakhtang Lejava, chief adviser to the prime minister.

Officials debated the approach to reforms in a series of meetings, many lasting late into the night. They first concluded that reform could not be piecemeal. The system was so corrupt, they believed, from top to bottom, that any attempt to introduce new recruits would fail, as new officers would soon succumb to the corrosive atmosphere of corruption. The unconventional idea of firing all 16,000 traffic police overnight was broached and debated. Some policy makers were concerned about what would happen to traffic safety after the police were fired and before the new patrol police could be hired and trained. The reformers realized that this concern was of little practical consequence, as the traffic police never really did anything to promote traffic safety; the only reason the traffic police stopped anyone was to get a bribe. Many worried about the reaction to a mass firing. In the end, the reformers believed it was the only way to begin establishing a credible and competent police force. So in perhaps the boldest move of the young government, in a single day, it fired and took off the streets 16,000 officers. To soften the blow, the government provided two months' pay and amnesty from past crimes. Some officers went without fuss; others joined the opposition. Chaos did not ensue—many observers believe that the roads were actually safer without the traffic people waving motorists over all the time—and a new patrol police force was created.

Zero tolerance did not stop with the firing of the traffic police and the hiring of new blood. Undercover officers were assigned to make sure the police followed the rules. An ordinary officer might be partnered with a covert officer and never know it—unless he or she broke a rule. Spot checks were carried out to make sure police were following protocol. An undercover agent filed a complaint of domestic violence at a police station to see if complaints were followed up on. A driver cruised around at night with a headlight out. When stopped, he would say he was on his way to fix the light and offer GEL 20. Police officers caught taking bribes were fired. Such practices sent a strong message to new recruits that the ministry was serious about its code of conduct and the ethical practices of its police.

To further protect citizens from abuse, the government introduced a 24-hour hotline that allows citizens to complain about police or report being asked for bribes. Video cameras went up all over Tbilisi, as well in other major cities and along highways, giving police and citizens proof of violations or evidence to the contrary. Fines were no longer collected on the spot but paid at commercial banks, eliminating opportunities for the police to pocket the money. Citizens finally had some leverage. They did not pay police directly and could report abuse and dispute fines through official channels. To eliminate petty corruption at the ministry level, the government streamlined or eliminated unnecessary processes, often as a result of feedback and suggestions provided by lower-level staff. Police work was made paperless.

The patrol police reforms were not just about stamping out corruption; they were also about restoring credibility by transforming the once corrupt institution into a citizen-friendly service. As Minister of Internal Affairs Ivane Merabishvili says, "Police help people solve their problems. Changing citizen's attitude toward law enforcement agencies is quite easy: simply the attitude of law enforcement agencies towards citizens must be changed" (Alenova 2010). In addition to their traffic duties, the patrol police walk the streets and are responsible for security in Tbilisi's subway system. They are the first responders on most police calls and are the face of Georgia's community policing program. They are aided by a radio center that receives information about actual or potential problems directly from citizens (24/7) and channels this information to the appropriate departments within the Ministry of Internal Affairs or relevant government agencies outside the ministry. Much of the training patrol officers receive is on interacting with the public in a professional and courteous manner.

Overcoming capacity constraints. Creating a new, professional, service-oriented patrol police force required many new people, with new attitudes and new skills. Massive recruitment was needed. To attract a more professionalized force, one completely untainted by corruption, the government recruited many new officers from universities and graduate law programs and required them to pass an exam. Recruits underwent hasty training to learn basic policing work, protocol, and public communication. "We recruited the best and brightest, so they were easy to train," says Merabishvili. In August 2004, 2,400 new patrol police manned the streets. Initially, there were not enough police to work the entire country, so other law enforcement units helped cover the regions. Patrol police recruits were given a six-month probationary period.

The speedy training of patrolmen and women and their university backgrounds led some critics to label the new force overeducated but underskilled. Later, candidates with high school diplomas were also accepted into the force, and basic training was extended from two weeks to two months, with periodic refresher courses. As might be expected, some of the early hires did not work out and were replaced—some for accepting bribes or failing to follow protocol. Others allowed their positions—with their shiny cars and fine uniforms—to go to their heads; more than a few officers were fired for abuse of their positions.

Higher salaries and bonuses made it easier to recruit new police officers. Salaries of the new patrol police were raised to $400–$500 a month, a tenfold increase over the salaries of the traffic police they replaced.

The professional development of the patrol police remains an ongoing priority. The old police academy was dismantled, replaced with a new academy that offers both the two-month course for new recruits and ongoing in-service training, including English language courses.

Creating a new look. The new force looks nothing like the old one. Gone are the sloppy men wearing soiled Soviet-era uniforms—often seen thumbing a ride after their cars broke down. In their place is a younger, fitter force—including women (15 percent of the patrol police)—driving new cars equipped with the latest onboard computers and wearing uniforms that are so smart a rumor circulated they had been designed by Armani.

The overriding idea in all of these reforms was to clean up the image of the ministry and the police force. Even buildings were revamped to look more professional. About 60 police stations in Tbilisi and the regions were built or renovated to look more open and inviting, some with glass exteriors and bank teller–like windows, suggesting a more transparent era.

Communicating the change. In case anyone missed the changes, the ministry ran a public relations campaign aimed at further enamoring the public of its friendly and approachable police force. One ad showed a handsome policeman kissing his wife; another featured an adoring elderly woman cooking her police officer son breakfast before he raced off for duty. "We wanted to create new role models," explains Speaker of the Parliament Bakradze. "Before the Revolution, a survey of school kids revealed that the majority wanted to be thieves-in-law when they grew up. The change in attitude would start by destroying the symbol that the thief-in-law is a respected man who owns the best property and whose word matters. We demonstrated that he is not a respected man, that his words do not matter; he does not own property, and his place is in jail."

Revamping Procedures for Driver's Licenses and Car Registration

The new service mentality extended to revamping procedures for driver's licenses and car registration. Before reform, the process was chaotic, time consuming, and corrupted. Driver's licenses could be purchased for about $100 (though some argued that there was a discount if you knew how to drive). They were often given as birthday gifts.

The new government established vehicle service centers that provided one-stop shops for licenses and vehicle registration where the emphasis is on quick and courteous service. The process became so efficient that it spurred the development of a large used car market adjacent to the service center serving the Tbilisi area. Used cars imported from the United States, Europe, and elsewhere are brought to the market for sale and often re-exported to neighboring countries. The paper work to expedite the sales transaction can be completed in a matter of minutes. The market has been so successful that the re-export of used cars became Georgia's leading export in 2011. In October 2011, the government removed the requirement that drivers need to carry their driver's license when driving. The patrol police can easily check for the license electronically from their car by entering the driver's name and birth date into the onboard computer.

Results

Crime rates have dropped, corruption in the patrol police has declined, a service culture has been developed, trust has been restored, and an accountability framework for the patrol police has been strengthened. Perhaps most important, one of the most visible signs of corruption in Georgia has been removed.

Sharp Reduction in Crime Rates

Thieves-in-law no longer influence Georgian society. Indeed, they seem to have no place at all. "Before the Rose Revolution, the best car was the criminal's car—better than the state official's car—and the best houses were the criminals' houses," says Merabishvili. "Now it is absolutely different. They are sitting in prison. No one is listening to them, and businessmen and state servants have the good cars and houses." The 2011 Georgia Crime and Security Survey indicates that 70 percent of respondents believed the authority of the thieves-in-law had decreased significantly (GORBI 2011).

Reported crime decreased by more than half between 2006 and 2010 (figure 2.1), with the number of armed robberies dropping from 2,160 to 398 (figure 2.2). Georgians are now safely strolling the streets of Tbilisi day and night, with more than 95 percent feeling safe at all times (GORBI 2011). Among the 15 most problematic factors affecting business measured in the World Economic Forum's 2011 Global Competitiveness Index, crime and theft barely made a blip, with only 0.1 percent of respondents citing them as problems.

Figure 2.1   Reducing Crime by More than 50 Percent, 2006–10

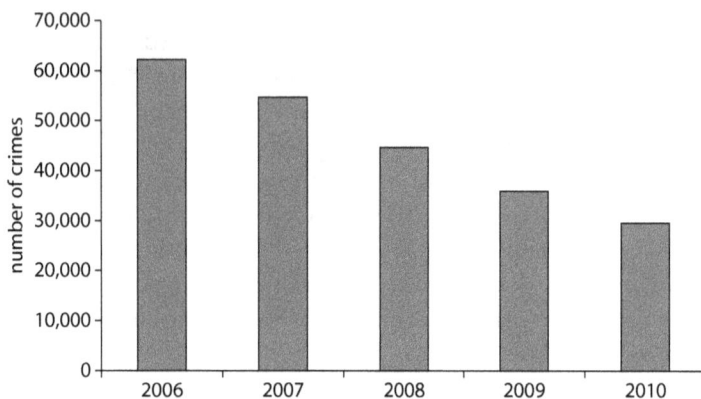

Source: Ministry of Justice of Georgia, 2011, "Seven Years that Changed Georgia."

Figure 2.2   Reducing Armed Robberies by 80 Percent, 2006–10

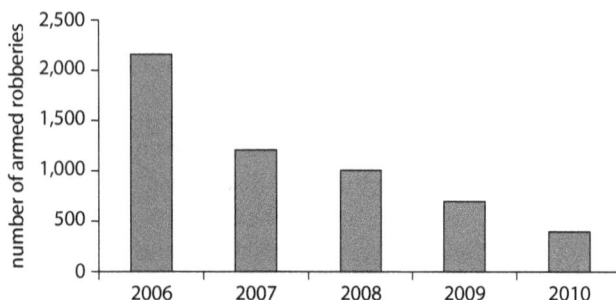

Source: Ministry of Justice of Georgia, 2011, "Seven Years that Changed Georgia."

Decline in Corruption

Corruption in the police force has fallen sharply, as several surveys reveal. A 2010 survey indicates that only 1 percent of Georgia's population reported having paid a bribe to the road police (World Bank and EBRD 2011). Comparable numbers were 30 percent in the former Soviet Union countries, 7 percent in the new member states of the European Union (EU), and zero in selected EU members (France, Germany, Italy, Sweden, the United Kingdom). Transparency International's 2010 Global Corruption Barometer shows that Georgia has one of the world's least corrupt police forces (figure 2.3). In fact, of all 86 countries surveyed, only Finland scored better than Georgia. Anecdotal evidence also suggests that the kind of petty corruption for which Georgian traffic police were once notorious no longer exists.

Creation of a Service Culture

A public service culture has been created in the patrol police, who are now considered friendly, courteous, and service oriented. They are trained to be helpful, and it shows. In the beginning, the change in attitude was novel. Motorists who had happened to stop alongside the road reported bracing themselves for the usual treatment when they saw a police officer approach the car and then being shocked when asked, "How can I help you?" The police are even deferential when writing traffic tickets. People wondered where these new police had come from, some joking that they must have come from another planet. Even drunk drivers are treated politely. When they are stopped, they are driven home rather than to the police station. Their car is impounded and they are charged, but they are treated with respect. Citizens have now grown to expect this new attitude.

Figure 2.3   Georgia: Forming One of the Least Corrupt Police Forces in Europe

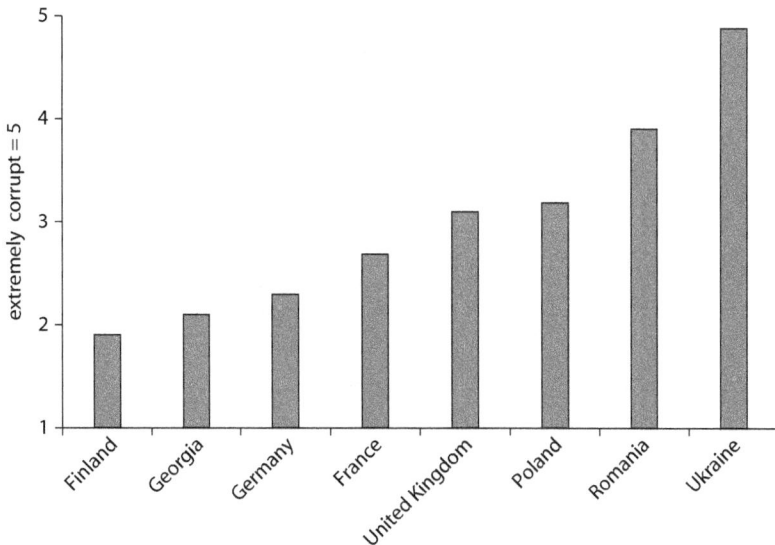

Source: Transparency International, 2010, *Global Corruption Barometer,* Table 2, pp. 42-43, Response to Question: "To what extent do you perceive the police to be affected by corruption?"

Increase in Trust

Trust in the patrol police has been created: 53 percent of respondents surveyed in the 2011 Crime and Security Survey assessed police work as good, and another 34 percent assessed it as fairly good (GORBI 2011). Similar results are found in an October 2010 poll by the International Republican Institute (IRI), which shows that 84 percent of respondents had confidence in the police, up from just 10 percent in 2003. A sociological study conducted by BCG Research in Tbilisi in January 2006 to assess public attitudes toward the police showed positive results (BCG Research 2006): more than 80 percent of respondents reported that police were friendly and oriented toward helping citizens; 55–60 percent described them as polite, fair, and responsible; and more than half noted respectful and cooperative attitudes between the police and citizens. Notably, 61 percent of respondents believed that police respected the law, and only 2 percent indicated that police were corrupt.

Stronger Accountability Framework

The accountability framework among the government, the traffic police, and citizens was transformed (figure 2.4). After ridding the ministry and its traffic police of corrupt individuals, reformers reduced the incentive for police to extract bribes and bully citizens by offering better wages (which increased by a factor of almost 10), training, and a

Figure 2.4   Accountability Framework for Patrol Police

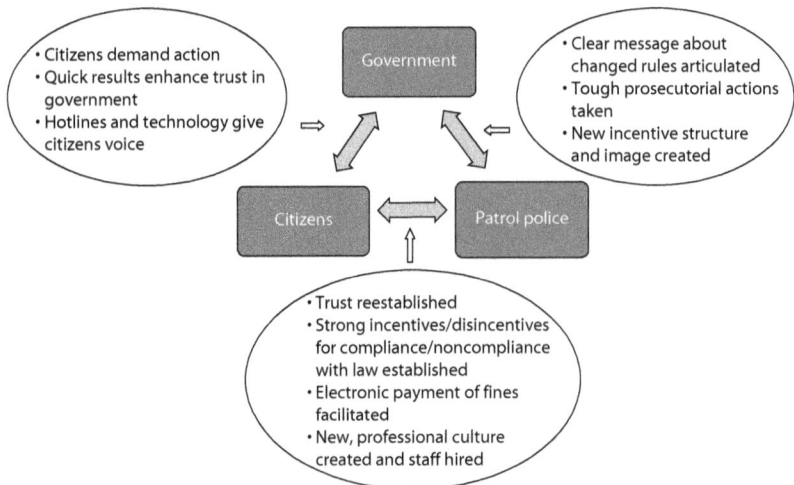

Source: Authors.

more professional environment. Police were incentivized to pursue genuine traffic violations and issue fines, the money from which went directly into ministry coffers and back into police salaries and benefits. At the same time, the reorganization of the ministry clarified the chain of command, and technology made following up on crimes more transparent and less open to corruption. The voices of citizens were heard; their distaste for corruption helped galvanize the sweeping reforms. Mechanisms such as the hotline, the video camera, and ongoing spot checks ensure that their voice will continue to be heard. In the end, a virtuous cycle replaced a vicious one.

Conclusions

The successful reform of the patrol police highlights several characteristics. The overnight sacking of 16,000 police officers established instant credibility in the government's reform effort. Trust was built with the deployment of a completely new patrol police and sustained by continued vigilance against corruption. Capacity constraints were overcome by intensive recruitment drives and an emphasis on continuous training and professional development. The nearly tenfold increase in salaries, the emphasis on developing a service culture, and the focus on professionalism all changed the incentive structure. The use of technology, such as the widespread adoption of traffic cameras and the electronic payment of fines, both enhanced police effectiveness and reduced opportunities for corruption. The media were used to communicate reforms and change the image of the police. The reforms are an ongoing process, requiring continuous vigilance by the authorities, as well as the involvement of citizens and the media in monitoring the performance of the patrol police and reporting problems to the authorities as they occur.

CHAPTER 3

Strengthening Tax Collection

The State of Affairs in 2003

The government's ability to collect taxes steadily deteriorated after the collapse of the Soviet regime. Increasingly sophisticated corruption schemes involving tax evasion, illegal tax credits, and outright theft of tax revenues resulted in perpetual collection shortfalls. Phantom revenues were booked as collected, so even when the budget indicated that funds were available, they often were not on the treasury's accounts. Tax authorities were openly criticized not only by opposition political parties but also by the donor community, the private sector, Parliament, and the National Bank, particularly just before the revolution. The inability of the leadership to control corruption—and in many cases, direct, high-level involvement in illegal deals—resulted in the accumulation of arrears for salaries, pensions, utilities, public works, and other state liabilities.

Georgia's first tax code was introduced in 1997. Considered a major reform at the time, the code, which included 12 state and 7 local taxes, turned out to be seriously flawed. The variety of taxes, complexity of accounting, and numerous exemptions and loopholes forced tax authorities to seek frequent amendments. More than 350 changes to the code were introduced between 1997 and 2003, making it extremely difficult for businesses to follow the frequent changes.

The complicated tax system created fertile ground for corruption, which often took the form of influence peddling by parliamentarians and senior government officials to obtain presidential decrees granting favorable tax treatment to favored companies. As many members of Parliament got elected to take advantage of parliamentary immunity from prosecution for criminal acts, exemptions often went to partners in crime. The tax authorities themselves granted arbitrary special exemptions to friends and political allies.

Bribery was also rampant. Businesses routinely paid bribes to receive favorable tax treatment and avoid punitive tax audits. These bribes lubricated negotiations between the tax authorities and business owners on what the final tax liability would be. It was easier for businesses and tax authorities to negotiate payments, including the amount to be paid in taxes and the amount to be paid in bribes, unofficially than to try to understand what the tax code actually required. A former deputy finance minister recalled one such negotiation, in a district of Tbilisi, that became so heated it ended with a tax inspector stabbing the company manager. As a result, all tax inspectors in the district were suspended for a month. Without the inspectors on duty, collections in the district were the highest ever recorded, as companies tried to figure out the best they could what they owed and paid it.

Corruption also included theft of government tax revenues. Many corruption schemes involved securing value added tax (VAT) refunds based on fraudulent transactions. Companies often end up paying excess VAT when they had extraordinary expenditures, such as construction. These excess VAT charges were recognized in the tax codes, and procedures were in place to refund the excess to the company. A typical scheme described by former finance minister Kakha Baindurashvili involved a paper trail of virtual taxes. A bogus company was established and a bogus paper trail indicating excess VAT payments created. The conspirators then collected the refund. In the most infamous case of virtual tax fraud, the head of the large taxpayers unit and a deputy minister of finance were prosecuted and convicted. Many other such fraud schemes went undetected.

Problems with the code fed into the overall atmosphere of corruption and dysfunction. Companies were compelled to cheat, and nearly all companies kept two sets of books, one for the tax authorities and one that reflected reality. Companies that were out of favor with the tax authorities or would not pay bribes faced constant harassment and were often forced to pay far more than they actually owed.

The result of this rampant corruption was increasing arrears on public goods and services, salaries, and pensions. In 2003, tax revenues officially represented just 14 percent of gross domestic product (GDP); in reality (after accounting for various offsets), the figure was even less (about 12 percent of GDP). The budget called for GEL 1 billion in revenue from all sources; the amount collected was only GEL 400 million. Funds to operate the ministries were routinely sequestered. Ministers spent much of their time lobbying the finance minister for funds, often to no avail. Ministries lucky enough to get an allocation often had to bribe Treasury officials to make the transfer. Pensioners went without pensions for months. When the new government took power, pensions were 18 months in arrears. Salaries had not been paid for many months either. Together with other overdue liabilities, arrears totaled more than GEL 400 million. Notions of public finance and tax compliance were largely nonexistent. In short, the tax system was thoroughly broken. As Baindurashvili notes, "Corruption was not ingrained in the culture. It was simply allowed to grow unchecked. It became an accepted way of life and everyone did it."

Post–2003 Anticorruption Reforms

The plundered treasury the new government inherited offered a stark and pragmatic reason to attack corruption forcefully and immediately. Zurab Zhvania, the newly appointed prime minister, approached Zurab Nogaideli about being finance minister the night after President Shevardnadze's resignation. There was no time to analyze the situation, he said, someone needed to begin taking action that very night. For taxes, the government launched a five-pronged approach involving altering the mindset, changing staff incentives, broadening the tax base, simplifying the tax legislation, and streamlining tax administration.

Altering the Mindset

The first step was to announce and enforce a policy of zero tolerance for corruption. The zero-tolerance policy was seared into the minds of the public and civil service. The police hit hard at well-known corrupt individuals. Television news captured scenes of masked and armed police forcibly closing down noncompliant businesses and arresting officials from the former government and other influential people. Among those arrested were the minister of energy and the minister of transport and communication, the chairman of the Chamber of Control, and the head of the civil aviation administration, the chief of the state-owned railway company, the president of the football federation, the president of the state-owned gold-mining company, and some oligarchs.

Those arrested could buy their freedom through controversial plea bargain arrangements that stretched the limits of existing laws. The government extracted significant resources from those arrested to begin replenishing the empty treasury account. One plea bargain with a prominent businessman resulted in a $14 million payment to the treasury. Although these arrangements let those arrested buy their freedom, they also sent an unequivocal message that even the powerful would be punished and that corruption would no longer be tolerated.

New laws were quickly adopted to reinforce the zero-tolerance policy. These laws simplified procedures for arresting officials suspected of corruption and allowed for confiscation of their property if they could not prove they acquired it legally. The government also approved tax amnesty legislation at the end of 2004 that allowed all taxpayers except government officials to declare all unreported assets before the end of 2005. Declared property could be legalized after the owners paid 1 percent of its cost to the budget.

Changing Staff Incentives

The zero-tolerance messages were not lost on people working in the tax department. Part of the immediate challenge facing government officials was that they could not fire and replace every tax collector and inspector, even though most had been corrupted under the previous regime. The immediate answer to this dilemma was to leave no doubt in their minds that the rules of the game had changed. Nogaideli recalls meeting with the staff of the tax department the night he was appointed finance minister. "I really didn't have the luxury to change staff beginning that particular night. I told them my judgment of their performance would not be on what they did in the past but how they performed in the coming months." Staff who continued with past practices were dealt with forcefully. Arrests and harsh sentences for corrupt tax collectors and inspectors quickly diminished corruption. Later, cameras were installed in tax offices to deter corruption. A room in the ministry was equipped with a wall of video screens showing every tax office in the country. Such scrutiny minimized the possibility for tax officers to cut side deals with taxpayers. Target volumes of collections were set and carefully monitored. Failure to meet targets was not taken lightly. As revenues increased, salaries were raised substantially, further decreasing incentives for bribe taking. Gradually, over a two-year period, new, better-educated, and less corruption-prone staff were recruited, eventually replacing the carry-overs from the previous regime.

Simplifying the Tax Code and Broadening the Tax Base
A new tax code was passed in 2005. The main goals were to stimulate economic growth, improve the efficiency of the tax system, and broaden the tax base, but the changes also had an anticorruption element, as the complexity of the old system created a medium in which corruption schemes could flourish. The new code simplified the tax system; reduced rates; and eliminated the pollution, property transfer, gambling, tourism, advertisement, and other minor local taxes, which had been bringing in almost no revenue. Only 7 of 21 taxes remained, with the rates of many of them reduced. The social tax rate was reduced from 33 percent to 20 percent, the income (payroll) tax was reduced from a progressive rate of up to 20 percent to a flat 12 percent, and the VAT was reduced from 20 percent to 18 percent. Remaining taxes included taxes on profits and property; excise taxes on alcohol, petroleum products, tobacco, and cars; and customs duty.

Rates were further reduced over time, so that by 2010, Georgia's tax regime was rated as one of the most liberal taxation systems in the world, with a combined personal income and social tax of 20 percent, a corporate profit tax of 15 percent, and a VAT of 18 percent—all of them flat taxes. The revenue lost from lower tax rates was largely made up through the broader tax base, better compliance, and stricter enforcement, including high fees and penalties for noncompliance. By removing most tax-payer exemptions, the legislative changes helped introduce uniform and equal treatment for businesses and expanded the tax base.

Measures were also undertaken to shrink the burgeoning gray economy and broaden the tax base. A controversial step involved shutting down the operations of small street vendors, who were unlicensed, operated informally, and did not pay taxes. An army of unhappy traders went to the streets to protest losing what for many was their sole source of income. The vendors had little public support, however; removing them resulted in less congested and cleaner streets and spurred the growth of small shops operating out of the shadows with much better services and sanitary conditions.

Another controversial measure was the requirement that every commercial establishment purchase and operate electronic cash registers that recorded the VAT collected on each transaction. Businesses were reluctant to buy relatively expensive equipment, and they balked at recording every transaction. Despite their protests, however, there was no compromise, no exceptions were made, and enforcement was strict. The tax department deployed phantom customers, often pensioners or pregnant women, throughout the country to check compliance with the new requirements. Shops failing to use the cash registers or provide receipts were fined heavily, with fines multiplying for subsequent infractions. Eventually, the new rules were accepted, but only because no one was exempted and everyone was treated equally.

Streamlining Tax Administration

Along with simplifying the tax code, the government sought to make it easy to file and pay taxes, in order to improve the business environment and reduce corruption. Filing tax returns was simplified by changing the filing dates for all monthly declarations to the 15th of each month. The new code also abolished the requirement of having an independent audit conduct annual filings. It abolished the rule of declaring current payables if there were no profits in the previous year. It also combined the forms for filing income and social taxes and simplified the process for paying property tax, eliminating the 2 percent tax on property transfers that buyers had had to pay.

E-filing was one of the first electronic systems offered to the business community. Manual (hard copy) filing of taxes used to involve going to different offices to pay different taxes, increasing opportunities for bribes. To prevent such opportunities, in 2007 the government set up an e-filing system, which minimizes interaction between taxpayers and tax officers.

The shift to the electronic system at first faced resistance from businesses that still used double-bookkeeping practices, accountants who feared losing their jobs, and others, who resisted giving up the familiar and having to learn something new. But the government pushed ahead. In November 2009, the ministry unofficially—and controversially— simply stopped accepting hard copies of tax declarations. As a result, the number of e-filers increased rapidly during 2010, with about 80 percent of taxpayers complying with the new rules in just a few months (figure 3.1). The government also introduced a web-based registration and declaration interface.

The government introduced a simplified electronic tax registration system, simplified documentation requirements for VAT payments, streamlined tax payments through banks to ensure that cash was delivered quickly to the treasury and the payment recorded accurately in the revenue service data base, and allowed taxpayers who registered

Figure 3.1   Number and Percentage of Tax Returns Filed Electronically, January 2009–September 2010

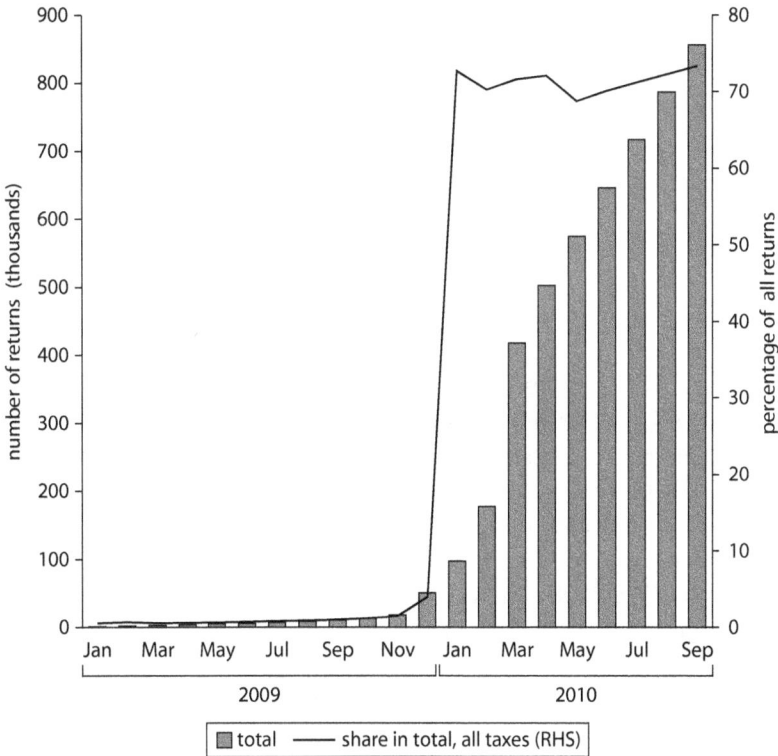

Source: Ministry of Finance of Georgia, Revenue Service.

electronically to access their account online. It also made substantial progress in reforming the accounting requirements for businesses.

The government also introduced risk-based management of tax audits. Under this approach, rather than target individuals and companies arbitrarily, the authorities target entities based on set criteria. The percentage of non-risk-based audits was reduced from 70 percent in 2009 to 35 percent in 2010 to zero in 2011. Recognizing that it lacks adequate in-house auditing capacity, in 2011 the government decided to allow companies to use private auditors to conduct tax audits.

A two-stage administrative dispute resolution mechanism was introduced to deal with taxpayer appeals, which now number more than 2,000 a year. About 30 percent of appeals cases have been resolved at the first stage of the process, an internal review of the case by a dispute council within the legal services department of the revenue administration headquarters. Disputes not resolved at this stage can either be submitted to a dispute resolution board chaired by the minister of finance or brought to court. Taxpayers do not have to pay the amount of tax under dispute until the case has been decided.

Results

Reform of taxation increased tax revenue, helping finance better service provision. It also reduced the tax and corruption burden on citizens and spurred the growth of business start-ups. As in other sectors, the key to success was a stronger accountability framework.

Increased Tax Revenue

The growth in nominal tax collection between 2003 and 2011 was remarkable across all taxes, with the largest increases in the profit tax (up by a factor of six), VAT and excise tax (up by a factor of more than five), and income and property tax (up by a factor of three). This expansion of the tax base was particularly striking given the sharp reduction in tax rates. The 2008 conflict and financial crisis negatively affected the revenue generation capacity of the economy, but revenues fully recovered by 2011.

The quick turnaround in revenue collection was particularly important in the days immediately following the Rose Revolution. By the end of January 2004, higher revenues allowed the government to pay all wages and pensions, something it had not done in years. By April, collections covered the entire month's budget requirement; by the end of June, a budget supplement was submitted to Parliament to obtain authorization to spend the GEL 200 million surplus over budgeted amounts to begin rehabilitating the power sector. By the end of 2004, collections had increased from 12 percent to 20 percent of GDP, reaching 26 percent by 2007 (figure 3.2).

Lower Tax and Corruption Burden

In 2009, *Forbes* ranked Georgia as having the fourth-lowest tax burden for businesses in the world—only Qatar, the United Arab Emirates, and Hong Kong SAR, China performed better (*Forbes* 2009). The tax wedge on labor cost measures the relative tax burden for an employed person. The average rate in the countries of the Organisation of Economic Co-operation and Development is about 36 percent—far higher than the

Figure 3.2   Tax Collections Increased, 2003–11

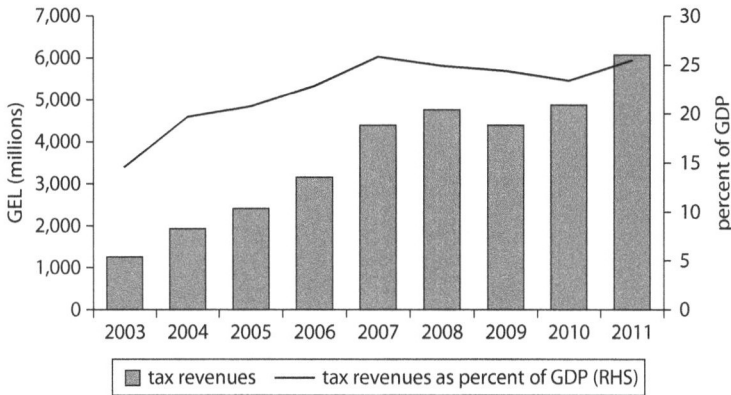

Source: Ministry of Finance of Georgia.

20 percent in Georgia. On the global *Doing Business* indicator of paying taxes, Georgia moved from 110th in 2005 to 39th place in 2012. The 2008 regional Business Environment and Enterprise Performance Survey (BEEPs) reports that only 3 percent of firms in Georgia reported that bribery was frequent when dealing with taxes—far lower than the 9 percent in the Europe and Central Asia region or the 18 percent average in the Commonwealth of Independent States. Georgia's performance represents a vast improvement over 2005, when 13 percent of firms reported corruption in the tax system (World Bank 2010b).

Increase in Business Start-Ups
The reduction of taxes and tax rates as well as the dramatic decrease in the amount needed to start a business (from GEL 2,000 to GEL 200) helped spur the creation of new businesses. By March 2011, more than 350,000 active businesses were registered in Georgia, up from about 205,000 in 2003. Many businesses also came out of the shadows, legalized their activities, and started to report actual employment volumes and costs.

Stronger Accountability Framework
Tax reforms succeeded in Georgia largely because of increases in accountability between principals and agents (figure 3.3). Changes in the tax code and legislation reflected the expectations of society in terms of rates,

Figure 3.3   Accountability Framework for Tax Collection

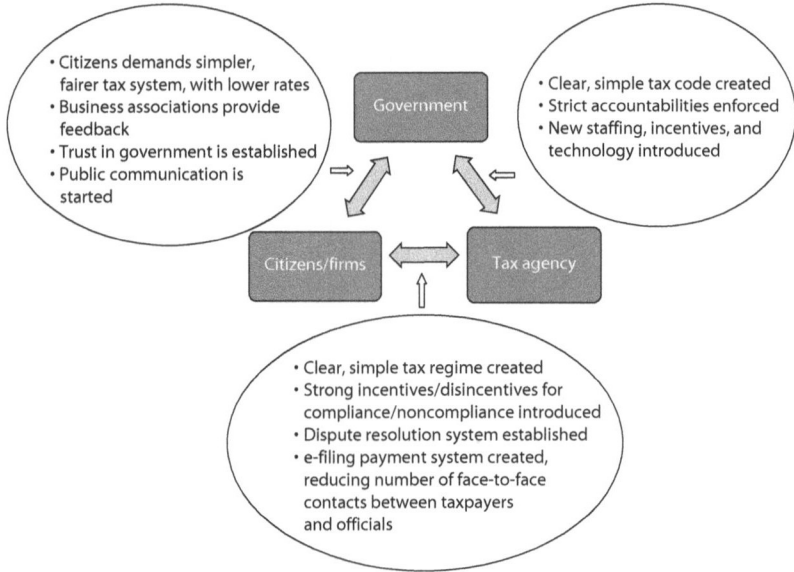

- Citizens demands simpler, fairer tax system, with lower rates
- Business associations provide feedback
- Trust in government is established
- Public communication is started

Government

- Clear, simple tax code created
- Strict accountabilities enforced
- New staffing, incentives, and technology introduced

Citizens/firms   Tax agency

- Clear, simple tax regime created
- Strong incentives/disincentives for compliance/noncompliance introduced
- Dispute resolution system established
- e-filing payment system created, reducing number of face-to-face contacts between taxpayers and officials

Source: Authors.

simplicity, and fairness. Under the new system, the revenue service (the agent) provides good-quality services through e-tools, including the e-filing system and e-declarations; a simple registration process; risk-based tax audits; and the tax appeal system. The client (the taxpayer) is convinced that taxes have to be paid. The overall tax burden is manageable, and the government is better able to provide public goods than it was before reform.

Conclusions

Government leaders shared a vision of the centrality of increasing tax revenues to restore the state. They understood that to boost revenues, the tax system needed to be much simpler and enforceable. They wanted a system that both provided revenues and was conducive to business development and economic growth. They established credibility early on, both through highly publicized arrests and by getting formerly corrupt tax officials to mend their ways. Foreign donor-financed tax advisers helped modernize the tax services, but many of the innovations and technology solutions adopted were home grown. As elsewhere in government, technology was used to both improve efficiency and reduce opportunities for corruption.

Sustaining improvements in tax collection remains a continuing challenge. Policy makers need to further strengthen revenue administration and deepen the new culture of public service to generate trust in a rules-based, objective enforcement of tax laws. At times, tax administration has been viewed as aggressive and sometimes arbitrary. New institutional arrangements to address these concerns—such as an appeals process and a dispute resolution board that includes a member of civil society—are steps toward strengthening the accountability framework.

CHAPTER 4

Cleaning Up Customs

The State of Affairs in 2003

Customs was yet another bastion of corruption. Borders were very porous and unprotected. Bribery and smuggling were the rule, not the exception. Anyone could bribe his way into the country with any kind of cargo and sell it without any record of import or payment of duty. Smugglers came on foot, by car, or by truck with bags of jeans from Turkey or food and fuel from Russia. Importing drugs, explosives, and weapons was more complicated (and required larger bribes), but bringing in virtually anything was possible.

There was no competitive recruitment or test of qualification to become a customs officer. Instead, prospective customs officers bribed officials to get their jobs—some paying up to $10,000. "Purchasing" a customs position was a good investment, which was soon recovered, as the palatial homes of many poorly paid customs officials suggested.

Although a customs code had been adopted in the early 1990s, enforcement remained weak and the code actually facilitated corruption. The multiplicity of rates—there were 16 categories ("bands"), with rates ranging from 0 to 30 percent—created a complicated system in which customs officials could abuse their power and extract bribes. Numerous exemptions created other opportunities for bribery.

Corruption was reflected in very low tax collection rates. Despite an average tariff of more than 20 percent, customs revenue collected represented less than 1 percent of gross domestic product (GDP), making Georgia's customs revenues among the lowest in the region.

Post–2003 Anticorruption Reforms

The reform of customs proved to be neither easy nor quick. According to former finance minister Kakha Baindurashvili, efforts were completed only in 2010. Even President Saakashvili was surprised by the eventual success of the reforms. "At the beginning I thought customs was hopeless," he said, "but I changed my mind now." In the end, customs reform was comprehensive, comprising changes in legislation, personnel, institutions, systems, and infrastructure. It was a process of fits and starts, with numerous setbacks along the way.

Strengthening and Simplifying the Legal Framework for Customs

One of the earliest tasks for the new government was to develop a new customs code. It set itself a one-year timeline—a timeline some international experts invited to help viewed as "mission impossible." The government had to deliver quick results and could not wait. It ended up developing a reform agenda largely in-house.

The new law on customs tariffs was introduced in September 2006. It eliminated the 16 customs bands, replacing them with a zero rate for 86 percent of imports and two other rates (5 percent and 12 percent) on a limited number of goods, such as agricultural products (designed to protect Georgian farmers). The law also equalized the customs treatment of World Trade Organization member and nonmember states, meaning that the same simple low tariffs applied to all. The import licensing system was simplified in 2005, when the number of licenses required for import and export was reduced from 14 main groups to 8, with licensing objectives limited to protecting public health, the environment, and national security (WTO 2010).

The customs code was amended in September 2009 and again as part of the 2010 tax reform. The amendments, which further simplified the customs process, achieved the following:

- Established a single revenue service that unified the tax and customs agencies and facilitated the use of a common identification system and sharing of data

- Reduced the number of documents required for customs clearance (excluding port activities) to four basic documents: declaration, bill of lading, power of attorney, and commercial invoice
- Reduced the number of documents required for export to two (export declaration and transportation document)
- Introduced a risk-management system, allowing customs services to target inspections on less than 10 percent of all cargo.

Replacing and Motivating Personnel

The reformers recognized that fine-tuning a legal framework would not make any difference without major changes in staffing and incentives. Most customs staff were corrupt and had to be let go. Doing so was not easy, as there was strong political pressure to protect many individuals. Initially, existing customs officers were trained, in the hope that they would change. "Understanding that rules and standards had changed and that corruption was not acceptable anymore did not come easily," however, according to Zurab Antelidze, who headed the customs service in the early years. The focus therefore shifted to bringing in new people. Some 80 percent of customs officials were ultimately fired, replaced with young, inexperienced staff.

Newly recruited staff were put through an extensive six-month training course. At the end of the course, the recruits were tested, with only the best selected for on-the-job training at customs checkpoints. Recruitment of good staff was made easier when salaries for customs officials were increased from GEL 30 to roughly GEL 800 a month over 2003–05.

Changing the Environment

Recruiting and training new staff and paying them well were still not enough to stamp out corruption. Changing the infrastructure at customs points was also necessary. The first checkpoint to be renovated and equipped with new equipment and staffed with newly recruited and trained staff was the Red Bridge post, on the border with Azerbaijan, in May 2005. The last checkpoints were renovated in 2010.

In an experiment, customs chief Antelidze compared the performance of new recruits sent to the renovated Red Bridge post with that of another group of new recruits sent to a post that lacked new facilities, equipment, systems, and procedures. He found that the group sent to the old style post—but not the group sent to the modern post—adopted the corrupt ways of the old customs officials. "It does not matter who you hire; what matters is the environment," he says. "What we learned is that we have to change the actors as well as the stage," added Vakhtang Lejava, chief adviser to the prime minister. Key to changing the environment at customs posts was enforcing zero tolerance for corruption where possible. To instill collective responsibility for fighting corruption, the customs service punished the entire shift when one customs officer was caught accepting bribes.

Even this was not enough to rid customs of corruption. The mindset of traders, who continued to offer bribes to customs officials, also had to be changed. To curtail bribery, customs officials posted announcements in multiple languages at customs points, stating that any attempt to bribe a Georgian customs official would be strictly punished, regardless of nationality. Dozens of citizens of neighboring countries caught trying to bribe customs officials were arrested, fined, and sentenced to a few days in jail. The action caused a brief diplomatic uproar, but it had the intended effect. Word quickly spread that the environment had indeed changed and that Georgian customs officials could not be bribed.

Reforming Institutions

Institutional chaos at the border the new government inherited slowed the reform of customs. Nine agencies operated at border posts—all of them corrupt and willing to collude to extort bribes from all who tried to pass. The new government was gradually able to reduce the number of services at the border to just two: the border (passport) control, under the Ministry of Internal Affairs, and the customs service, under the Ministry of Finance. Even this arrangement was unsatisfactory until 2008, when the patrol police replaced the corrupt border police who had been responsible for passport control. Even though they belonged to different ministries, the two services cooperate closely on logistics, sharing electronic databases. The officers of each service share cross-designation, meaning that customs officers can handle passport control and immigration officials can deal with customs documents. In 2009, the customs service was merged with the tax service into a single revenue service.

The early zeal to enforce zero tolerance reduced bribery, but it was not necessarily conducive to quick border crossings. In the beginning, the newly established financial police were posted at customs checkpoints to supervise the work of customs officers and make sure that no one violated the law or made mistakes. Zero tolerance for corruption meant that no distinctions were made between small mistakes and criminal offences: either could result in jail or high fines. In 2008, the financial police were relieved of their customs duties and cameras installed.

Archaic procedures exacerbated the problems at the border. For instance, valuation of goods for taxation purposes had been a major problem. In most cases, the invoice value of goods reported by importers differed significantly from the actual value. Customs officially were given discretion to valuate goods using methods that many importers found abusive. Initially, the value databases and methods were not sophisticated enough to provide for selectivity and objective judgment. This lack of adequate procedures, coupled with the intense scrutiny of the financial police, often slowed customs clearance to a crawl. Officers opened every single bag crossing the border, taxing more than was fair. A joke ran that if you had a pair of socks, one of the socks must be for sale.

The strict enforcement of rules sometimes created unexpected problems. For instance, the enforcement in 2004 of a 1990s rule that allowed importers to bring up to 20 kilograms of homogeneous goods into the country without full customs procedures and taxation led to large-scale abuse, as importers divided their shipments into numerous 20-kilogram packages and hired locals for GEL 2–3 to bring them across the border. Sometimes the local population aided smugglers by creating a disturbance to distract the financial police. In response to the problem, customs officials conducted more intensive searches, inspections, and passport checks, but this strict approach created frictions that eventually led to confrontations. The financial police and even special forces from the Ministry of Internal Affairs tried to protect the border, but fights occasionally broke out. The searches for smuggled items contributed to the already long queues, forcing importers with big trucks to spend up to a week waiting to cross the border. These delays created annoyance with the new system. The perception that it was no longer possible to smuggle goods into Georgia grew, but so did complaints about the unfriendly attitude of officials.

Gradually, institutional changes were implemented that eased and then eliminated the queues. A one-stop shop was put in place to minimize the physical interaction between customs officers and traders. Under the old system, importers had to go to different customs windows to process their goods. With the one-stop shop, they obtained all the documents they needed from a single window. The documents were assigned a number and processed in back offices, where contact between the importer and the customs official was not possible. This approach reduced the number of steps to clear customs, sped up the process, and limited opportunities for corruption.

Additional improvements to the system came in 2009, with the implementation of an automated risk-management system that classifies importers into risk categories based on 15 criteria. Low-risk clients are fast-tracked through customs, which limits discretion and simplifies processing. The system reduced the share of declarations going through the red (enhanced scrutiny) corridor from 15 percent in June 2009 to just 7 percent in June 2011. The risk-management software program also embeds criteria for selecting declarations for random checks, which are performed on 1–2 percent of declarations.

Three new customs clearance zones were established in 2010 to further streamline the customs clearance process, reduce the number of procedures and processing time, and improve customer satisfaction. Electronic declaration and advanced declaration were also introduced. Customs clearance no longer takes place at the border. For transit cargo, the border official (an immigration or customs officer) checks the driver's passport, the transit documents, and the seals on the truck, and, if all is in order, sends the truck on its way in a matter of minutes. For goods destined for Georgia, trucks are sent either to the designated custom clearance zones or, if advanced declarations were filed, directly to the importer's facilities, where the papers are processed.

Before reforms, private customs brokers and freight-forwarders helped traders complete customs procedures and provided warehousing services (as they do in most countries). Many of the private brokers were dismissed customs officials, whose presence created an opening through which corruption could seep back into the system. To deal with the problem, the government expanded the state presence, albeit in a business-friendly way. Initially, the reform envisaged eliminating the services of private brokerage companies; following the reaction of the private sector, however, the system of private brokers was retained. This new approach has been positively received by both Georgian businesses and non-Georgian trading partners.

Results

Georgia's customs now features state-of-the-art infrastructure, a strong client-oriented service, streamlined clearance, and successful implementation of integrated border management approaches, such as cross-designation of border officials, delegation of powers between agencies, and data sharing. Corruption, once widespread among customs and other border officials, is now under control, with a zero-tolerance policy, commitment of officials to transparency and integrity, and an operational layout that reduces opportunities for bribe payment and rent-seeking.

The reform process took nearly seven years and encountered numerous difficulties and setbacks along the way. Not until all staffing, institutional, infrastructure, and systems reforms were in place was success achieved, both in curbing corruption and improving the efficiency of the service. "Until then," noted former finance minister Baindurashvili, "the incompletely reformed system was like an octopus ensnarling everyone in the tentacles of corruption."

Better Overall Performance

Reform significantly liberalized trade: by 2010, Georgia had the fifth lowest average tariff of 181 countries and the lowest barriers to trade in its region (Europe and Central Asia) and country income category (lower-middle-income). The share of goods with zero tariff (86 percent) is the highest in the region and among the highest in Georgia's income group. Georgia ranks third in the General Agreement on Tarriff and Trade's Commitment Index, a measure of commitment to liberalization of multilateral services (World Bank 2010a). The volume of trade has plummeted, and customs revenue has increased (table 4.1).

Stronger Accountability Framework

Early on, the government signaled its zero-tolerance policy, passed legislation that liberalized the trade regime, implemented personnel changes, and improved staff incentives (figure 4.1). Institutional changes and improvements in infrastructure and systems took longer, both for political reasons and because of cost, but they have been part of a holistic effort to address corruption in customs.

Table 4.1   Selected Indicators of Customs Performance, 2003–10

Indicator	2003	2008	2009	2010
Revenue ($ million)	202	1,199	958	908
Customs staff	1,320	969	1,101	1,168
Annual number of declarations	75,252	204,556	162,353	183,862
Revenue collected/customs staff ($)	153,530	1,237,358	870,118	777,397
Trade volume (m)	1,603	7,901	5,840	6,602
Declarations/staff	57	211	147	157

Source: World Bank staff calculations, based on data from the Ministry of Finance.

Figure 4.1   Accountability Framework for Customs

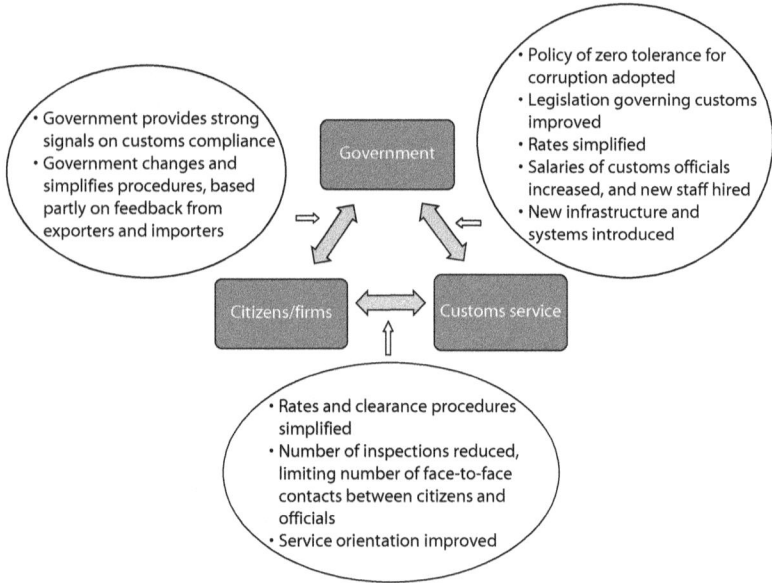

Government

- Policy of zero tolerance for corruption adopted
- Legislation governing customs improved
- Rates simplified
- Salaries of customs officials increased, and new staff hired
- New infrastructure and systems introduced

- Government provides strong signals on customs compliance
- Government changes and simplifies procedures, based partly on feedback from exporters and importers

Citizens/firms

Customs service

- Rates and clearance procedures simplified
- Number of inspections reduced, limiting number of face-to-face contacts between citizens and officials
- Service orientation improved

Source: Authors.

Conclusions

Doggedness in maintaining zero tolerance of corruption was key to the success of customs reform, which included simplification of the import regime, modernization of procedures, and transformation of the customs service. The struggle to establish credibility took longer than in other areas, but the government's persistence eventually paid off. Recruiting and training new staff, raising salaries, and heavily investing in new technologies and facilities were all critical. But at the heart of the success were the institutional changes that changed the incentives and the rules of the game and strengthened the accountability framework, essential for the sustainability of these reforms.

CHAPTER 5

Ensuring Reliable Power Supply

The State of Affairs in 2003

By 2000, Georgia's power sector teetered on the edge of collapse. A decade of financial mismanagement, pervasive corruption, and even sabotage of power stations had left much of the country literally in the dark. Although power lines stretched into remote mountain villages—connecting 95 percent of the population—no part of the country had power around the clock, and some areas went without electricity for days. Even in Tbilisi, power was available only about seven hours a day on average.

Electricity in Georgia was traditionally supplied by local generation (hydro and thermal) and imports from what had been the Soviet Union. Georgia generated excess power in the summer, when rivers filled with water flowing from the snowcapped Caucasus Mountains. Under the Soviet regime, Georgia exported the excess power through a unified Soviet grid in exchange for winter imports. After independence, trading excess summer power for winter imports became unreliable, because of supply shortages and problems in making payments.

By 2000, power generation had fallen to half of 1990 levels. Some facilities had broken down completely and no longer supplied power. Those remaining were highly erratic, leading to frequent countrywide blackouts that brought Georgia to a standstill. Unreliable power made even taking the metro dangerous, as underground trains would stop in total darkness, with only emergency lights illuminating the cars. Hopelessness with the power situation had reached such a point that demonstrations in Tbilisi were not about the fact that the power was usually out but about trying to get some advance notice of when it would be on.

Power shortages also resulted from sloppy management and electricity theft. Inaccurate measurement of consumption, a chaotic billing system, and failure by many customers to pay led to a shortage of funds for facility maintenance. Electricity theft was widespread. Single power poles would be festooned with hundreds of wires illegally connecting lines reputed to have reliable power to nearby homes and businesses. Theft from lines connecting hospitals, the metro system, factories, and even neighbors' generators was common.

Corruption permeated every stage of operation, including generation, transmission, and retail and wholesale supply. Power company officials negotiated import contracts behind closed doors under murky circumstances, often using multiple middlemen. The parties actually selling the power and the prices and terms of the contracts were rarely disclosed. Ministry officials routinely sold on the black market diesel fuel meant to run power plants in the winter months. Consumers frequently paid bribes to power company employees to get lower charges or free connections or to connect their homes to the power supply of a local hospital or factory; some risked getting electrocuted trying to make the connections themselves. Utility workers paid kickbacks to their supervisors to keep their jobs. Cash collections were a mere 25–30 percent of billable amounts.

Payment discipline was also compromised by lack of metering, a legacy from the Soviet era; frustration with poor service reliability; and chaotic billing practices. Power companies did not always issue receipts or record transactions. People who got receipts kept them, because without company records, distributors assumed people had not paid and billed them again.

Corruption drained the sector of funds and caused distribution companies to regularly default on tax payments. Power companies were highly indebted to the state, their accounts sometimes seized by tax authorities. As a result, payments to suppliers, service providers, and collections were all cash based. Large amounts of cash changed hands, with few records or receipts to track cash flow. Some of this cash was used to supplement salaries or meet other needs of the power companies, but cash-strapped power companies did not always pay salaries, leading some staff to solicit bribes to earn a living.

Utility employees were not the only ones who accepted bribes in return for promises of reliable power supplies or for turning a blind eye to illegal connections. People affiliated with power companies, such as law enforcement agents and government officials, also did so. In the regions, the head of police, the governor, and the head of the prosecutor's office all needed money. According to Prime Minister Nika Gilauri, their main source of income was the power sector.

Post–2003 Anticorruption Reforms

The power sector reforms pursued by the government beginning in 2005 were holistic and aimed at quick results that would build a virtuous cycle of political support. They focused on restoring financial discipline and promoting investments to increase capacity, reduce technical losses, and improve service reliability. To push them through, in 2005, the government established a state energy commission, chaired by the prime minister, which initially met twice a week.

Improving Financial Discipline

The government instilled financial discipline by restructuring and privatizing the power sector, strengthening cash collections, and bringing in a new team to manage the power ministry. Improving cash collections and eliminating the problem of nonpayment required four main steps. First, the staff of state-owned distribution companies were held accountable for collections—a move that led to the prosecution of corrupt officials and the firing of some 3,000 of about 20,000 staff in 2004–05. Financial incentives were also introduced. In the 54 business units in the sector responsible for collections, for instance, the top 10 percent were given bonuses and the bottom 20 percent were fired.[1] Efforts to improve cash collections were also supported through media campaigns.

Second, thousands of electricity meters were installed to link consumption directly with billing. Ideally, every house, apartment, and business would have been metered, so that individual consumption could be measured, but the government had neither had the time nor the money to do so. Where individualized metering was not possible, collective meters were installed. Groups of houses or apartment buildings were connected to a meter that measured total consumption for the group, which then had to figure out how to divide the bill and collect the money. If the group failed to pay the bill, all units under the collective meter were cut off. The use of collective meters was instrumental in raising collection rates quickly. There were instances, however, where disputes over electricity bills among neighbors on the same meter ended in unrest and required police intervention. In addition to the meters, a new electronic billing system was introduced that allowed consumers to pay their bills at banks or online. The new system eliminated cash collections, reducing opportunities for bribery and theft.

Third, to show that the rules of the game had indeed changed, the government disconnected prominent nonpayers, such as the Poti Water Utility, the Tbilisi trolleybus company, and the Tbilisi General Hospital. For Prime Minister Gilauri, who was energy minister then, "Disconnecting the hospital was a difficult decision, but it worked, and the hospital management paid its arrears in a few hours." Disconnecting the power sent a strong message to all nonpaying consumers that the rules of the game had changed, that everyone now had to pay for power.

Fourth, tariffs were raised, in steps, to cost-recovery levels. This increase in tariffs would not have been possible if Georgia's citizens had not seen commensurate improvements in power supply. For former prime minister Zurab Nogaideli, "Total reform was only possible when the President realized that the political price of higher tariffs was less than the political cost of no electricity." To soften the blow of higher tariffs, especially on the poor, the government introduced a new social protection program under which all consumers received a one-time electricity voucher worth GEL 50. It also introduced lifeline tariffs, targeting the poor, which provided a basic consumption threshold.

Privatizing Power

To boost efficiency and profitability, the government implemented a plan aimed at privatizing the sector, which had already been unbundled into generation, transmission, and distribution companies. Initially, two competing strategies emerged, one put forth by Nika Gilauri, the other by Kakha Bendukidze, who was then minister of economy. Both strategies shared the same goals, of providing around-the-clock electricity supplies to the entire country and making the power sector financially sustainable. They differed in how to achieve them. Bendukidze favored rebundling the sector and privatizing distribution and generation into four vertically integrated companies. Gilauri's program, dubbed the Program for Lighting Georgia, called for making initial state investments in the unbundled companies, clearing up their debts, restoring them to financial viability, and then privatizing them.

The second plan won out.[3] The state made significant investments ($300 million from the state budget, along with substantial financing from donors) in the sector, rehabilitating hydropower and thermal power stations. A debt-restructuring plan with external suppliers was also worked out to bring the utilities' balance sheets back to health. The government also suspended the operations of several small distribution companies, which had few customers and were sources of corruption.

Subsequently, private participation was attracted to the sector. Privatization was seen as an instrument with which to fight corruption and ensure efficiency in the sector. Power sector entities that were privatized included the United Energy Distribution Company, which supplies power to all consumers outside Tbilisi, and six hydropower stations.

Changing the Team

For Gilauri, the most difficult challenge was building a new, reform-minded team that could implement the needed reforms for "young, educated, hard-working people, with a mix of experience and youth." He involved himself in the hiring of not only deputy ministers and heads of departments but also lower-level professionals. Key to hiring and retaining staff was paying them attractive salaries. Higher salaries became possible as tax collections increased and the financial strength of the power utilities improved.

Results

Reforms in the power sector achieved remarkable results, transforming a totally corrupt sector with a crumbling infrastructure into a financially stable net exporter of electricity and a potential source for new investment and growth. Many people, including some in government, believed that these results would never be achieved. Prime Minister Gilauri recalls a discussion he had in 2005, when, as minister of energy, he asked his deputy to create a balance sheet for electricity supply and demand that was realistic and based on round-the-clock electricity supply. His deputy responded, "Why do you want us to work for nothing? We can create the balance sheet, but 24/7 supply is not possible in Georgia ever." The deputy was soon proven wrong.

Improved Power Sector Performance

Within a very short period of time, reformers completely turned around Georgia's power sector:

- Power is now available around the clock. No nationwide blackouts were reported over 2009–11.
- Technical losses in the transmission system declined from 6.6 percent in 2004 to 1.7 percent in 2010.
- Collections increased from 22 percent of billings in 2004 to 95 percent in 2007 and 100 percent in 2009 and 2010.
- Tariff rates are at cost-recovery levels.
- Higher tariffs and collections forced households and businesses to improve consumption efficiency. Consumption in 2010 was only 8 percent higher than in 2004, despite the fact that electricity is now supplied around the clock.
- Domestic power generation increased from 6.9 TWh in 2004 to 10.0 TWh in 2010.
- Georgia, a net importer of power in 2003, is now a net exporter.

Stronger Accountability Framework

Before the Rose Revolution, there was little accountability in the sector. Corruption perpetuated nonpayment, lack of financial discipline, and overconsumption, all of which contributed to a shortage of electricity. The old government instructed distribution companies to keep electricity supplied at all costs. As power companies rarely disconnected customers for nonpayment, there was no accountability between consumers and service providers. A key driver for achieving results has been the strengthened accountability in the sector (figure 5.1).

Conclusions

Zero tolerance for nonpayment of electricity was essential to establishing credibility very early on in the reform process. The government was committed to disconnect nonpayers no matter who they were—hospitals, army bases, even state prisons. No payment meant no electricity, without exception. The government's guarantee and subsequent delivery of 24/7 supply strengthened the credibility of reform. Similar disconnection efforts before the revolution had not been effective, because the power company had not been able to provide around-the-clock service for paying customers. The decision to adopt communal metering was an unconventional solution to

Figure 5.1   Accountability Framework for the Power Supply Reliability

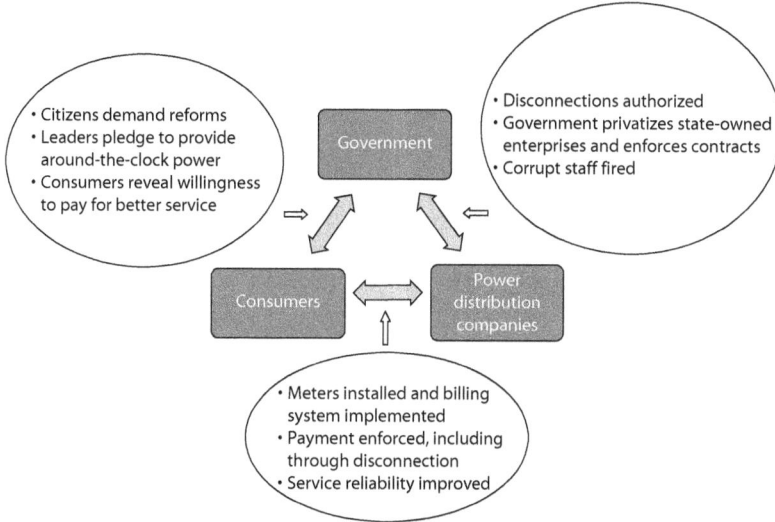

- Citizens demand reforms
- Leaders pledge to provide around-the-clock power
- Consumers reveal willingness to pay for better service

Government

- Disconnections authorized
- Government privatizes state-owned enterprises and enforces contracts
- Corrupt staff fired

Consumers

Power distribution companies

- Meters installed and billing system implemented
- Payment enforced, including through disconnection
- Service reliability improved

Source: Authors.

getting payments up quickly. By charging communities with responsibility for collecting payments and disconnecting blocks (or entire villages) if payments were not made, the government made it clear that the rules of the game had changed. Installing thousands of new meters and rolling out a new billing system were key tools for eradicating corruption within the distribution company. The billing system not only measured electricity consumption and issued bills, it also monitored abnormalities in the electricity bills that could have been caused by corruption.

CHAPTER 6

Deregulating Businesses

The State of Affairs in 2003

Before reforms, Georgian businesses were mired in government red tape, and executives were regularly harassed by corrupt officials. More than 900 business activities required a license or permit, and dozens of inspections were conducted monthly and annually in which inspectors looked mostly to line their own pockets. Dealing with government requirements was time consuming, confusing, and costly. People needing permits or licenses stood for hours in government agencies only to be told to come back later or to fill out paper applications that wound up in boxes barely accessible by officials, much less the public. Procedures were labyrinthine. Getting a construction permit involved 29 procedures, with approvals from as many as 9 agencies. Completing the process could take the better part of a year. Even officials had trouble following procedures, which they would sometimes simply make up. Many companies operated outside the law. Less than 45 percent of construction projects had legal permits (World Bank, *Doing Business* 2005).

The slow and confusing system fostered corruption. People paid bribes to obtain permits more quickly or circumvent license requirements. Corruption ran all the way to the top. "If someone wanted to export scrap metal," says Vakhtang Lejava, chief adviser to the prime minister, "he paid thousands of dollars to the minister of the economy. The size of the bribe depended on the volume of the export." To add a floor to an apartment building, builders paid about $50,000 to a zoning regulatory official. "Everything cost money," he notes, "and it went right into officials' pockets."

Corruption was not a secret. Drivers bribed emissions testers to get a passing emissions certificate, even when their car was spewing smoke. The fire inspectorate operated out of a shell of a building with dilapidated cars out front. "The fire inspectorate was the funniest," recalls Lily Begiashvili, deputy head of revenue service at the Ministry of Finance and a former deputy minister for reforms coordination. "Imagine the guy who does absolutely nothing in his life. That was the fire inspector. He just comes to work and plays cards." In fact, many inspectors did get out of the office—to collect money and distribute it among colleagues.

Post–2003 Anticorruption Reforms

Reformers slashed business regulations, eliminating entire agencies that served no legitimate purpose or were unable to implement their mission because of capacity constraints. They created one-stop shops, cut processing times, reduced the number of inspections, adopted "regulatory outsourcing," and revitalized staffing in an effort to improve the business environment and lighten the regulatory burden on individuals and firms.

Applying the "Guillotine"

In 2005, Kakha Bendukidze, then the minister of the economy, started an aggressive reform project to dramatically cut licenses and permits and to simplify procedures to make Georgia attractive to local and foreign investors. "You can't have a 1,000-day plan," he notes. "You have to strike when the opportunity presents itself." That opportunity came when Georgia's president asked him to take a look at deregulation. The ministries had prepared an initial list of regulations to look at for reform, but the list was a short one, prepared as it was by the very people who had an interest in maintaining the status quo.

A staunch libertarian, Bendukidze believed in limited government. He recruited Vakhtang Lejava and Lily Begiashvili, both of whom shared his passion for reform, to lead the review of regulations and licenses with him. To conduct the underlying analysis, he recruited a cadre of enthusiastic young people, most of them in their 20s and early 30s, who were untainted by Communist ideology and shared his vision of small government. They operated under the theory that corruption happens when citizens come in contact with state officials. Even with good policing, every interaction cannot be monitored. The approach was therefore to limit contact between citizens and the state, as reformers in other sectors had done. They believed that most regulations, and the agencies behind them, were not working anyway, so that eliminating them would simply remove channels of corruption. Bendukidze believed that "you couldn't make things worse by eliminating an agency that has no capacity to do its job and only issues worthless pieces of paper in return for a bribe."

The group drew up a list of agencies, along with every license, permit, and inspection each required. They analyzed the impact of removing various requirements and studied practices in other countries. In some instances, they determined that the license or permit served no legitimate role. In other instances, they decided that the regulation might produce a public good—controlling auto emission, for example—but that corruption was so endemic that the inspection or permit did not have the intended effect.

Before final decisions were made, state officials had their say. They met with the team to defend regulations they believed were necessary to reduce risks to health, safety, and the environment and to demonstrate that their agency had the capacity to administer and enforce them. "You can have a license with a noble goal," says Lejava. "But it doesn't mean the capacity exists to reduce risks."

Mid-level bureaucrats typically represented their ministries before Bendukidze's group. The meetings were often tense and emotional. Some presenters resorted to claiming that major catastrophe would ensue in the absence of their permits or licenses. During one discussion, a health ministry official broke down and cried. A conversation with the agency responsible for regulating the pharmaceutical sector deteriorated into a shouting match.

Within a few weeks, the team sent Georgia's cabinet of ministers a list of permits and licenses they recommended scrapping. Soon after, in June 2005, a law was passed that clearly defined all types of activities that required a license or permit, slashing their numbers by 84 percent, from 909 to 145, and then later to 137, removing vast well-exploited opportunities for corruption along the way.

Of the 137 licenses and permits remaining, most regulate activities potentially threatening to human health, the environment, or national security, such as medical-related activities and dual-purpose goods like chemicals used in both weapons and industrial production. Applying for these licenses and permits became simpler and faster and now involves less face-to-face contact between state officials and citizens.

The new rules were changed many times as the government sought to improve them or remedy shortcomings. The changes sometimes led to confusion among businesspeople. The construction permit system, for instance, was amended 16 times in the three years following the initial reform. "Fine-tuning of reforms was and remains the rule, not the exception," explains Lejava. "The reality with significant reforms is that you see the biggest problems at first, but then when reforms are tested in reality, you see underlying issues."

Perhaps because the reforms were drastic and constantly changed, communications to the public were often inadequate. As a result, many businesses continued to apply for licenses that were no longer required. A year after taxi permits were eliminated, for example, "entrepreneurs" were still selling them, and ill-informed drivers kept buying them. "The biggest mistake the government made was not communicating its reforms in the right way," notes head of state procurement agency Tato Urjumelashvili, who helped draft the legislation on deregulation. "They did a lot of good things—they made life easier in many ways—but they didn't communicate that." Others expressed similar sentiments in interviews.

Creating One-Stop Shops

To simplify procedures, the government created one-stop shops. Citizens now go to one office within each issuing ministry to submit their documents, and the issuing agency, not the applicant, is responsible for collecting relevant information from other government agencies. All fees are paid through banks, not to officials.

Processes were automated, with applications entered into a transparent computer system. Business processes for issuing licenses and permits were spelled out in staff guidelines and, where possible, computerized, with time limits imposed for the completion of each step. There would be no more tossing applications on shelves and forgetting about them.

Each ministry will ultimately have its own service center—many in their own building—to administer and provide licenses and permits, thereby separating the policy-making bodies from the units administering and issuing the permits and licenses. This work is ongoing. Ultimately, a larger system will link service units from different ministries.

To speed up the application process, the government eliminated unnecessary bureaucratic steps, such as the mandatory registration of company charters—which few people ever understood how to do. Applicants who register in person at the issuing agency no longer have to get documents notarized.

In construction, an industry once fraught with corruption, a new regulation reduced the number and types of structures requiring permits (eliminating the need for permits for buildings less than 100 square meters, for example). Most of the approvals required from various agencies to obtain a construction permit were eliminated (figure 6.1).

The vast majority of businesses in Georgia no longer require any kind of permit or license to operate. Business owners still register a new business with business registry and tax authorities, but the process has been dramatically simplified. Before reform, businesses were required to register separately for business and tax purposes—a requirement that involved two separate and largely redundant paper-based processes in two locations, resulting in two unique identification numbers. The process took weeks and required eight documents, notarization, payment of minimum capital, and the creation of an official company seal. Georgia's rank rose sharply on *Doing Business* indicators related to anticorruption (figure 6.2).

In 2007, the government unified tax and business registration, making only one registration necessary. In 2010, the public registry agency took over this role. Tax registry remains with the Ministry of Finance. However,

Figure 6.1   Sharp Decrease in Number of Official Procedures Needed to Build a Warehouse and Number of Days to Complete Them, 2005–10

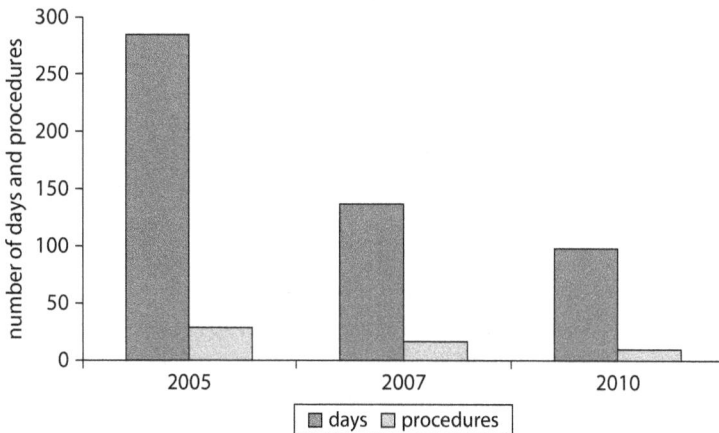

Source: World Bank *Doing Business.*

Figure 6.2   Georgia's Rank in Key Anticorruption-Related Reforms in *Doing Business* Indicators, 2005 and 2011

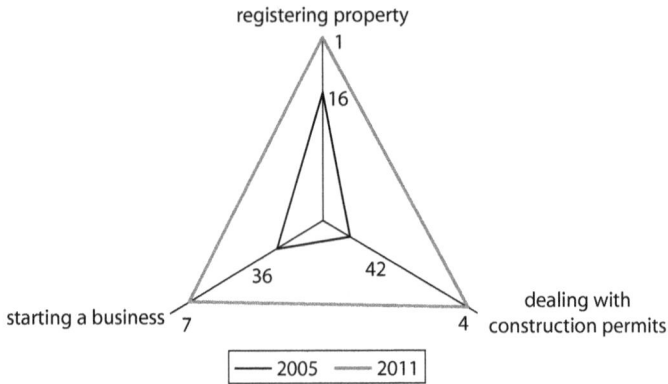

registering property

1

16

starting a business 7   36   42   4   dealing with
                                                    construction permits

—— 2005   —— 2011

Source: World Bank *Doing Business.*

when companies register with the public registry agency, they automatically receive a tax registration identification number, which is the same as the business registration number. For most businesses, the only documents required to register are an application and proof of payment of registration fees. The entire process can be completed in a single day.

Cutting Processing Times

To accelerate processing, reformers introduced the concept of "silence is consent." Departments were obliged to issue most licenses in 30 days and most permits in 20 days or give a clear explanation of why they did not. If a question about an application remained or more work was required, the deadline could be extended up to six months. However, if the applicant failed to hear anything within the prescribed time limit, the application requirements were assumed to have been met and the license or permit was deemed to have been granted. If mistakes were made along the way, the responsibility fell on the state official who may have failed to properly perform his or her job.

Of course, implementation was not without problems. Ministry employees who lacked the training and experience to meet the new deadlines were suddenly expected to process applications quickly. Some applications were approved by default that probably would not have been if the deadlines had been met. Despite teething pains, the discipline of the "silence is consent" approach was revolutionary in making services responsive to consumers.

Where possible, private sector service providers have replaced state services to increase efficiency. Private sector engineers accredited by the ministry have replaced the state workers who once rendered second opinions on safety and structural issues related to complicated constructions, for example. The idea is that private inspectors will compete to build reputations and be less inclined to take bribes.

Reducing the Number of Inspection Agencies

Reforms reduced the number of inspection agencies from 40 in 2005 to about 20 in 2011. If an inspection, permit, or license system was failing because of corruption, it was eliminated; once capacity improved, it could be reinstated. Based on this rule, food safety and fire inspections were abolished. Fire inspections have been partly revived and integrated into emergency services under the Ministry of Internal Affairs; some elements of sanitary inspections, conducted by state officials and private inspection companies, are also being reintroduced. Fewer inspections has meant fewer bribes, as public officials have limited opportunities to extort money for services they may not even have provided.

Adopting "Regulatory Outsourcing"

Former prime minister Lado Gurgenidze emphasizes another form of regulatory simplification adopted by the government, which he calls "regulatory outsourcing" (Gurgenidze 2009). Many goods and services that have undergone regulatory scrutiny in an Organization for Economic Cooperation and Development (OECD) country do not need to be recertified in Georgia. A financial institution with a license issued by an OECD country can establish a branch in Georgia and notify the national bank without prior approval. Consumer goods, including food, certified in any OECD country can be imported without further certification. Pharmaceutical products licensed in the European Union (EU) or in another industrial country also require no Georgian license.

The same approach applies to technical standards and codes. All standards or codes adopted in EU, other OECD, or Commonwealth of Independent States countries have been adopted in Georgia in parallel with local standards and codes. Relying on the regulations of countries with greater regulatory capacity reduces bureaucracy and limits opportunities for corruption in Georgia.

Revitalizing Staffing

As in other sectors, institutions and staff were overhauled. Whole ministries were eliminated or folded into other ministries, based on the idea that excessive bureaucracy increased the risk of corruption. Between 2004 and 2005, nearly 28,000 civil servants lost their jobs, according to government figures.

"When you have lots of employees you need to keep busy, they create work for themselves," explains Bendukidze. "They created regulations to justify jobs. Initially, the intention was not necessarily corrupt, but the regulations created opportunities for corruption to emerge."

Better training and higher salaries were offered to officials who stayed—some experienced staff were retained to run divisions—and to recently recruited younger staff. The average salary of public officials in construction licensing, for example, increased by a factor of 20 (from GEL 15–20 a month in 2004 to GEL 300–400 in 2006), further undermining the incentive to solicit or accept bribes.

Results

Georgia has emerged as a global leader in deregulating businesses and improving its business environment. Both are essential features of a small open economy whose future is inextricably linked to its ability to attract foreign investment in a competitive world.

Higher Doing Business Rankings

Georgia shot up in the *Doing Business* rankings, from 112th in 2005 to 16th in 2012 (World Bank 2012). It did particularly well in the rankings most closely related to anticorruption reforms: registering property, dealing with construction permits, and starting a business. Direct correlations between better *Doing Business* rankings and higher foreign direct investment or growth are difficult to determine because of the economic shocks from the August 2008 conflict and the global economic crisis of 2008–11. But international evidence suggests that countries with higher rankings attract more foreign investment and grow faster. The improvements in Georgia have laid the basis for both as the global economic environment improves.

Stronger Accountability Framework

Perhaps the most striking reform to the business environment was the reform in thinking: getting government officials in a post-Soviet country to reduce the size of their agencies and their own influence. This change of mindset is an enduring legacy of these reforms and a central feature of the accountability framework (figure 6.3). It is key to holding agencies accountable for the services they provide.

Reforms did away with most public providers that could not prove their worth or contract out services to the private sector. The focus was on setting performance standards for remaining service providers and simplifying processes. Adopting the principle of "silence is consent" and introducing one-stop shops were major innovations that tightened the accountability framework.

The reforms were made possible in part because of widespread disgust with the status quo. The government was able to tap into the population's deep-seated desire to get rid of corruption to push through dramatic reforms despite an entrenched bureaucracy. But it could have done a better job of informing citizens about the design and extent of changes that were actually implemented.

Conclusions

The ambitious deregulation of business dramatically reduced corruption and simplified life for business owners and managers. Some 95 percent of businesses no longer need any kind of permit or license. Interaction with

Figure 6.3   Accountability Framework for Licenses and Permits

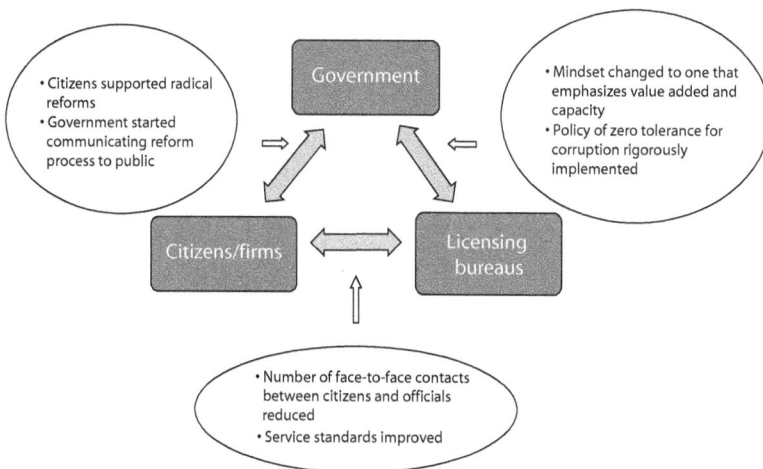

Source: Authors.

officials over licenses and permits is limited, and all interactions are recorded electronically. Most ordinary citizens will never require a license or permit, unless they build a house—typically a once-in-a-lifetime kind of event. Obtaining permits and licenses has become much faster as well, decreasing the incentive to pay bribes to accelerate the process.

Several factors explain the success of business deregulation. The most important may be the fact that the reformers shared a vision of limited government and believed that reducing contact between the state and its citizens was key to the fight against corruption. Bendukidze was perhaps the most fervent proponent of this approach, and he converted many in government to his view. The deregulation reforms radically altered the incentive structure. Agencies were assessed by the value added they provided and the capacity they had to carry out their role.

The reform process was unconventional. It included a cadre of young, committed staff recruited on short-term contracts to research the regulatory structure of other countries and prepare meticulously for the grueling "guillotine" meetings with agency after agency. These meetings represented a novel approach to regulatory review that put the burden of proof on the agencies to show their worth. The process benefited from lessons from other countries, particularly those with a similar view of the limits of government, including Estonia, New Zealand, and Singapore.

Not all facets of reform were successful. The government did not always do a good job of communicating about reforms, and it overestimated the capacity of agencies to adapt quickly to the requirements of one-stop shops and the "silence is consent" rule. These weaknesses notwithstanding, of all the anticorruption reforms implemented by government, the systematic review and reform of business regulations stands among the most audacious and successful.

CHAPTER 7

Making Public and Civil Registries Work

The State of Affairs in 2003

Systems for registering anything from a birth certificate to a new business were chaotic and corrupt. Inaccurate information was stored in Soviet-era archives. Registering a property involved trips to various offices for stamps and signatures and notarizations on pieces of paper that were filed away. Responses often took up to two months. To obtain a passport, citizens went to one office, only to be sent to another to get proof of residency before returning to the first office to stand in line for hours to bribe some official just to do his or her job.

Communication between agencies—such as the business and civil registries, which stored related data—was largely nonexistent. Agency officials made little effort to share information, leading to mistakes and duplication of work, as well as higher costs and longer delays. Registering property involved eight procedures, took on average 39 days, and cost about 2.5 percent of the property's value, according to a 2005 World Bank *Doing Business* report.

Fees for services were not posted—or even written down—creating fertile ground for corruption. The price to register property, for example, could be based on transaction size, value, or whatever officials felt like charging. At property registries, hundreds of people would jam into small, smoky offices hours before the office opened—and then wait in line for five or six hours. Corruption was rampant. Entrepreneurial types would join the queue to sell their spots to latecomers. Private brokers walked around helping people move transactions—for a fee. Citizens paid to speed up the process at the property registry or to buy fake registrations or permissions. They paid state workers to survey their properties. Failure to pay could mean never having a proper cadastral survey conducted.

Officials were often on the take, requesting unnecessary and hard-to-obtain supporting documents to extract bribes even from powerful people with political connections. Authorities also demanded money to help people prepare documents and navigate the confusing process—a service not officially offered.

Corruption at registries was so blatant that criminals used civil registry offices to buy passports in different names. Even regular citizens used the registries to illegally change information on their documents, including single women and athletes who changed their ages to make people believe they were younger.

Cash from bribes was divided among various officials, including the police. Officials working at civil registry offices paid $5,000–$25,000 to get their jobs. Some people obtained lower-level jobs by giving a television or a refrigerator to the hiring official. Ironically, a 2004 survey on public perceptions related to paying bribes to tax authorities, customs officials, police, and public registry agents revealed that although respondents found most bribe-takers offensive, they were grateful to public registry officials for registering their property (Georgian Young Lawyers' Association 2005).

Post–2003 Anticorruption Reforms

Making registries work required building institutions and simplifying processes as well as attracting and retaining new staff. The use of information technology was key to these efforts.

Building Institutions and Simplifying Processes

Even before the time the new government came to office, it was clear that the rules of the game had to be changed. A working group (supported by the donor community and nongovernmental organizations) had created a plan for a transparent, self-financing public registry with friendly customer service, simplified procedures, and clear user fees. But the plan had failed, because of a lack of political will and the vested interests of government and public registry officials. In February 2004, many of the people from the earlier working group came together to put their ideas into action. David Egiashvili, a lawyer and participant in the 2002 working group, led the team.

The group spent 10 months drafting new legislation, focusing first on legal and institutional issues. In June 2004, Parliament approved the Law on State Registry, which dissolved the public registry agency, a decentralized body with supervisory responsibility that was undermined by the competing and conflicting interests of local governments, land committees, and councils. The law created the National Agency of Public Registry (NAPR), a legal entity under the ministry of justice. Set up to provide quick and easy access to public registry information, the new self-financing registry would offer simplified registration procedures, secure ownership rights, and customer-friendly service, ultimately stimulating economic growth.

"Before the reforms, the public registry was underfunded, because it received money from the state budget. The first thing we did was to change the system," says Zurab Adeishvili, the minister of justice. "We have transformed the corrupt bureaucracy into a business model that generates 10 times more income and provides efficient services to citizens. Now we have about 1,000 motivated people working in the property registry. They earn their salaries and contribute to the state budget."

According to reform team leader David Egiashvili, the second step was to remove conflicts of interest by restructuring the roles and responsibilities of various agencies handling public registry issues. Under the old system, for example, registrars were responsible not just for registering property but also for monitoring land use and ultimately selling state land, creating an obvious conflict of interest. The new law prohibits registrars from being members of a commission selling land. The monitoring role went to municipalities, which lost the power to help choose regional registrars, power that had led to political influence over land valuations, registrations, and disputes.

Anything that smacked of corruption was cut. Top people lost their official cars. Nine offices that coordinated registries at the regional level were eliminated. "When we analyzed their function, we saw that most of their activity was about coordinating corruption," said Egiashvili. The Bureaus of Technical Inventory, which registered buildings in urban areas and handled surveys and land cadastre, was also disbanded, replaced by private surveyors. Today, some 25 companies compete in this business, keeping costs in line with market demand and leaving little room for corruption.

What remained were the central body (the NAPR) and 68 registry offices around the country, all connected to one computer system. Maintenance of all information, as well as procurement, accounting, and payroll functions (previously handled locally and leading to misappropriation of funds) would be handled centrally, with regional offices registering property. "We needed to change the mentality," says Egiashvili. "Registrars were to sit in an office, look at documents submitted, and decide to register them or not. They weren't there to monitor anything in the field."

The number of documents required to register property was reduced from six to two and later one (the sales and purchase agreement). The simpler system cut unnecessary steps such as the mandatory notarization of sales agreements. In its place, parties now register agreements by signing them at the agency. Property can now be registered at any of the 500 authorized users of NAPR software, including notaries, banks, and real estate companies.

"When I was appointed, I was given two assignments," says Egiashvili. "The first was 'no corruption' and the other was 'no queues.'" Cutting procedures helped shorten queues, as did adding a separate information counter to handle simple questions (before reform, 70 percent of people standing in line needed nothing more than questions answered).

In 2004, the government created the Civil Registry Agency, a self-funding public entity under the Ministry of Justice. The new agency is responsible for passports; identification cards; birth, death, and marriage certificates; citizenship and migration issues; and the legalization of foreign documents—work previously handled by 78 local offices.

New legislation cut red tape. It streamlined the procedures required to obtain civil registry documents and required that officials, not citizens, track down necessary documents kept by their agency and others. "If information is stored in a government agency, our employees can't ask citizens for it," says Giorgi Vashadze, deputy justice minister and head of the civil registry. Databases from various agencies are now unified online, allowing these documents to be accessed in seconds.

All fees charged by the Civil Registry Agency are now clear and in writing—as are the time frames for issuing various documents. In some cases, processes that used to involve bribes were simply formalized and made legal. For example, for a fee, citizens can get documents processed the same day—much like they used to pay bribes to speed things up.

"We analyzed the structure of corruption related to the timeline of registration and said, let's just replace it with fees for service," said Egiashvili. An identification card, for example, is issued in 10 days at no charge or in 1 day for a fee of GEL 25. Delivery times have been dramatically cut. For a fee, passports can now be obtained within 24 hours; other documents, including birth, death, and marriage certificates, can be issued within 15 minutes. Georgia even offers VIP service, in which an agency official will show up at a citizen's office with a portable workstation to process a passport application.

Like other public agencies, public registry offices do not accept fees directly. Instead, commercial banks or bank representatives present at these offices collect these fees, limiting the ability of public officials to extract bribes. Front and back offices are separated physically and functionally, meaning citizens could no longer sit around smoking with and chatting up (or paying off) back-office workers involved in decision making. Officials working in front offices were trained to be friendlier to applicants and taught when to get a supervisor. Local civil registry agency offices were revamped with glass windows, bright lighting, and staff assigned to greet customers and answer their questions.

Attracting and Retaining New Staff

At both the public and civil registries, restaffing was a priority. The new system called for a fresh way of thinking: registrars would be processors of documents, not arbiters of power. Changing the mentality of registry officials was not always possible. As a result, many had to be laid off. At the end of 2004, all 2,200 public registry employees were fired in a single day. Most were invited to reapply for their jobs, which involved taking an exam. A few thousand candidates interviewed for 630 positions. About 400 of the old guard, mostly in the regions, kept their jobs.[4]

At the civil registry, more than 400 new employees were immediately recruited after passing exams that tested knowledge of civil registry procedures, new legislation, and computer and other skills. All staff had to reapply for their jobs and take the tests. Most failed. They knew the old practices but not the proper way of doing things. Over time, some 80 percent of the original staff has been replaced.

New people were recruited through advertising campaigns aimed at attracting highly skilled professionals. Salaries for public registry workers increased by a factor of almost 20—from about $20 per month in 2003 to about $400 in 2005, creating intense competition for jobs and reducing the incentive to accept bribes. Training and workshops were added to upgrade staff skills, along with a new incentive scheme that provided performance bonuses equal to up to two months of wages. The Ministry of Justice, the parent ministry of both the civil and public registries, created a new center that trains registry officials.

Similar incentive systems were implemented at the civil registry. Midlevel employees under the old regime earned an average of $15 a month. The new agency immediately boosted their monthly salaries to $200 and later $500. A new bonus scheme was introduced, along with team-building workshops and customer service seminars.

Along with improved incentives, the government introduced a system for monitoring performance. "Mystery shoppers" were used to grade services and check for corruption at both registries. They also made sure employees were following procedures. At the civil registry, the results of these visits are factored into employee reviews, leading to bonuses, more training, and even dismissals. A hotline enables citizens to report illegal actions of agency officials. It also allows people applying for jobs to complain if they feel they have been unfairly treated.

Harnessing Information Technology

As it did with other reforms, information technology (IT) played a critical role. A team of 10 programmers designed a public registry system to transparently track the flow of documents. According to Egiashvili, some IT specialists earned more than he did. "I was not happy about it," he said, "but it was good for the software development." The system is used by regional offices and can be accessed by its 500 authorized users and, to some extent, the public. It is searchable by name, address, cadastral code, registration number, and other fields.

Digitizing old Soviet archival records and cadastre information from every property registry office has been a monumental task. The database includes satellite images, digital maps, and cadastral information and is linked to other government agencies, including the Ministry of Finance and the Civil Registry. When an NAPR registrar enters a citizen's or business's identification number, name and address information is automatically filled in from the civil registry and business registry databases. In 2010, the business registry became part of the NAPR.

At the civil registry, major technological changes were introduced over time. Before reform, about 10 computers served the entire civil registry, and identification cards were typed using a typewriter. Today, agency employees have their own computers, which are linked to an agencywide system that records all activities, making them transparent.

All offices of the civil registry are connected technologically as well, making it possible for citizens to request documents from any civil registry office, not just the one at which they registered their documents. Diplomatic missions and consular posts are also connected to this database.

Progress has also been made with Internet services. Georgians can obtain their passports overseas without visiting a consulate. Identity is confirmed during a video call with face recognition software using photographs from documents issued since 1993. The database already includes some 9 million photos. The new system also makes it easier to identify falsified documents.

Before 2005, some 70 percent of citizens still held Soviet-issued passports. Many people never bothered to register deaths, because it was a hassle or because their family preferred to keep pension payments coming. Legislation passed in 2011 made it mandatory for medical institutions to send messages about births and deaths electronically to the agency within five working days or be fined GEL 500.

Underpinning reforms has been a big push to create complete electronic pictures of every citizen. Civil registry employees have been going village to village and to schools with portable kits and cameras to register citizens and issue free identification cards. Citizens have been informed that failure to secure a proper identification card within a year would mean a loss of government benefits. Today, some 97 percent of the population have photo identification cards, which are linked in the agency's database to documents such as birth certificates and residency permits, some digitized from old paper records.

In April 2010, the government introduced passports that include biometric data, photos, fingerprints, and digital signatures. More than 184,000 of these passports have been issued. Passports will automatically be linked to a new kind of e-identification card, introduced in the summer of 2011. This secure card will include a digital signature; biographical data, such as name, date of birth, and fingerprints; as well as bank account and employee verification information. It will serve as a tool for receiving public services. The new cards are not obligatory, although the old cards will no longer be issued.

Integrating Service Innovation
In 2011, the government opened the first four public service halls, in Batumi, Kutaisi, Mestia, and Rustavi. These new institutions go one step beyond the one-stop shop idea by allowing citizens to access services

from various agencies under a single roof. Citizens can register property or businesses; obtain identifications, passports, and birth and death certificates; and get notary services at a public service hall. Self-service areas are available for a number of simple transactions; customers are directed either to quick service areas for simple questions or to operator desks for tasks that will take more than five minutes. Each hall is brightly decorated and has staffed areas where children can be entertained while their parents complete their business. Comfortable waiting areas are available with free Internet connections. A greeter meets people at the entrance and guides them to the right place. Employees are intensively trained, not only in the technicalities of their work but on creating a friendly, customer-oriented environment. Interestingly, the idea for the public service hall originated at a management retreat held by the Ministry of Justice. The focus of the retreat was on how agencies can improve services, reduce delays, and make bureaucratic processes as painless as possible.

Learning from International Experience

The new Georgian public registry system incorporated lessons learned from other countries, such as Lithuania, as well as from international workshops and donor community experts. Reformers paid special attention to examples from foreign banks and other private sector entities. "We took the best of what we learned from all of them," says Egiashvili, "but we didn't copy any one system. The vision was our own."

Civil registry reformers also turned to international experts. The United States and the European Union paid for study tours to countries in the Baltics and Europe, where Georgian officials studied best practices. The European Union funded a Hungarian expert to work with a team of Georgian lawyers to visit local offices to see how civil registry agencies operated and come up with new ideas. The overriding goal was to create agencies that were not just free of corruption but operated more like commercial entities than bureaucratic government bodies.

Changes of this magnitude typically take many years to implement. In Georgia, a team worked 12-hour days and made massive changes right away—later going back and tweaking them. As expected, developing software, implementing procurement, and instituting new procedures to speedily produce passports was not easy. Rapidly creating the database, for example, was difficult, and the initial version was not very sophisticated.

Communicating with the Public

Creating public awareness is a critical part of reforms. Frequent press conferences are needed to tout new services, booklets outlining services must be distributed in villages and schools, and meetings with citizens must be held to explain plans and get feedback. Initially, reforms were communicated poorly. In 2005, shortly after reforms started, long lines of people wanting identity cards and passports plagued agency offices. The newly recruited employees were not yet ready to handle demand. Word had circulated that a speedy new service had been introduced with set fees, but many citizens feared that in six months' time, civil registry officials would probably go back to the old corrupt way of doing things.

The government has dramatically improved the way it communicates reforms to the public since the contentious 2008 elections, according to Lily Begiashvili, the deputy head of the revenue service. "After the elections, the government understood very well that without any public information or public information campaign on these issues, success would be lost." Government officials now host public events to talk about new services and use television, radio, and the Internet to explain them. All ministries and government agencies have public relations consultants, whose jobs are partly devoted to communicating government reforms. Still lacking are detailed guides for entrepreneurs that explain licensing and permitting regulations.

Results

The results of the reform of Georgia's public and civil registries are obvious to ordinary citizens. Corruption, chaos, and inefficiency are gone, replaced by service-oriented employees at facilities that are welcoming, brightly lit, and comfortable. Bribes are neither demanded nor accepted. Procedures are clear, with set fees and timetables, and transparent via computer. Several key results stand out.

Establishment of a New System for Property Registration

A secure system for registering property rights was established. Trust in the new system is illustrated by the significant increase in property registrations between 2003 and 2010 (figure 7.1).

Increased Business Efficiency

The time, effort, and costs of accessing various public services have fallen sharply. Registering property, which took 39 days in 2005, now

Figure 7.1   Increase in Number of Property Registrations, 2003–10

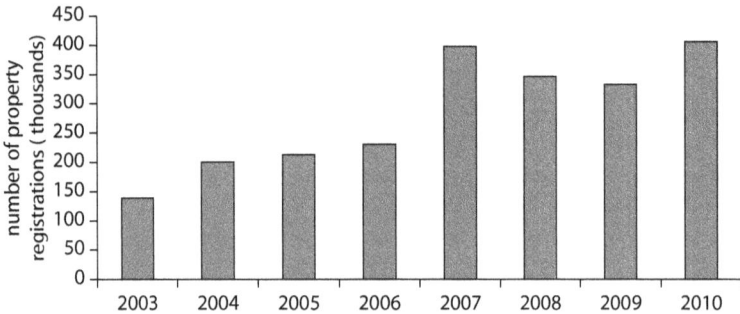

Source: National Agency of Public Registry.

takes just 2 days, and the cost of doing so fell from 2.5 percent of the property value to 0.1 percent. The number of procedures has been cut from 8 to 1. As a result, Georgia now ranks first in the world in terms of ease of registering property, according to the 2012 *Doing Business* report. New public service halls provide an array of public services under one roof, and most services can be accessed online, even from abroad. Improvements in efficiency have been supported by a self-funding model that has enabled the registries to increase their revenues, become financially viable, and improve the services they provide. This model has increased the budget of the public registry agency from about $300,000 in 2004 to $7 million in 2006 and about $25 million in 2011.

Greater Trust in Registries

Trust in the registries has improved dramatically. A public opinion poll taken in 2004 indicated that 97 percent of Georgians believed the civil registry was one of the most corrupt agencies in the country. A similar survey conducted at the end of 2006 showed a total reversal of opinion: 97 percent of respondents believed that there was no corruption in the agency. These results were confirmed by the 2010 Life in Transition survey, which indicated that only 1 percent of respondents felt that unofficial payments were needed to obtain official documents—about the same as in advanced European Union countries (World Bank and EBRD 2011).

Stronger Accountability Framework

Reforming the public and civil registries involved creating a new service-oriented mindset. By ending budgetary support, the government forced the agencies to become self-sufficient. Reforms eliminated many functions with the potential for conflict of interest. Agencies were no longer permitted to monitor land use; other services, such as land surveying, were privatized. The agencies' processes were simplified, streamlined, and in some cases eliminated. Transparent technology and the separation of front- and back-office functions removed back-office influence over registrations, making bribes unnecessary. Higher salaries, better incentives, and the use of mystery shoppers have made taking bribes less appealing. At the same time, staff gained influence over their organization's fate through their independence from other ministries and increased responsibility to provide better service and boost revenues. Citizens gained power through simplified procedures, access to clear guidelines on timelines and fees, and a hotline for reporting abuse. All these features have strengthened the links of accountability among the government, the registry agencies, and citizens (figure 7.2).

Figure 7.2   Accountability Framework for Public and Civil Registries

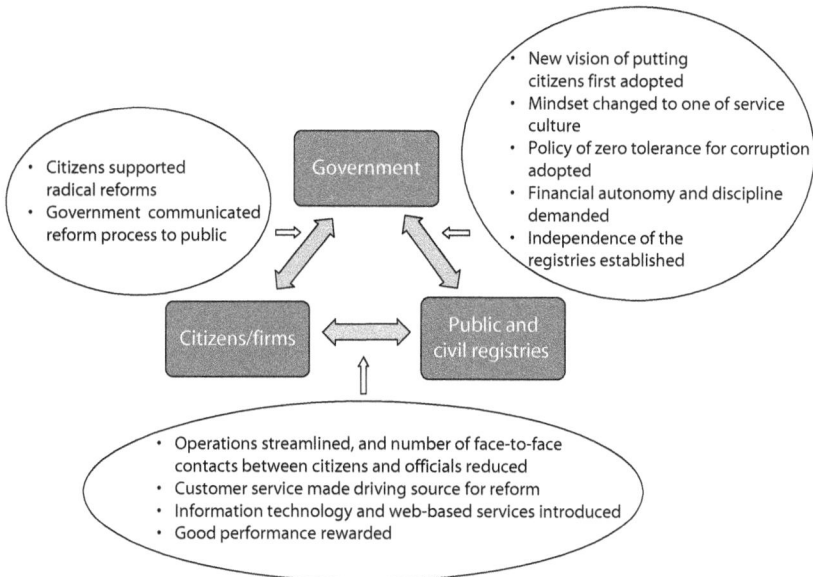

- New vision of putting citizens first adopted
- Mindset changed to one of service culture
- Policy of zero tolerance for corruption adopted
- Financial autonomy and discipline demanded
- Independence of the registries established

- Citizens supported radical reforms
- Government communicated reform process to public

Government

Citizens/firms

Public and civil registries

- Operations streamlined, and number of face-to-face contacts between citizens and officials reduced
- Customer service made driving source for reform
- Information technology and web-based services introduced
- Good performance rewarded

Source: Authors.

Conclusions

Reform of the registries stemmed from a clear vision on cleaning up the interface between citizens and the state and creating service-driven agencies, as well as from the zero tolerance for corruption that drove other public service reforms. Financial autonomy, higher salaries and opportunities for bonuses, and training and professionalization changed the incentive structure within the registries. The new salary structure enabled the agencies to compete for good staff, alleviating capacity constraints. Simplified procedures and the widespread adoption of new technologies were also key factors in the success of the reforms.

CHAPTER 8

Rooting Out Corruption in University Entrance Examinations

The State of Affairs in 2003

Education funding in Georgia dried up following the collapse of the Soviet Union. By the time of the Rose Revolution, all educational institutions suffered from a lack of books, barely qualified teachers, and crumbling infrastructures. Salaries were so low—a university professor earned about GEL 60 a month in 2002, less than half the minimum subsistence level—that bribe taking was considered an acceptable way to get by.

Students paid bribes to get into universities, to pass exams, and to get their diplomas. Although the quality of education was usually poor, having a university degree conferred a certain social status and granted access to jobs.

The university admission system was considered the most corrupt area in higher education. Theoretically, candidates were accepted solely on their performance on university entrance examinations. In practice, a system of patronage permeated the entire process, with university presidents admitting the sons and daughters of politicians in exchange for political support. Other students got in by bribing middlemen—little-known university professors or school employees who were responsible for collecting money and passing it upward to influential university staff and members of the examination panels. Outstanding students were usually able to pass the university entrance exams and gain admission based on their knowledge and performance, but many other students got in based solely on their ability to pay bribes. Some newly established private institutions were actually diploma mills, typically run out of small apartments with a single "professor."

Bribes ranged from $8,000 to $30,000, depending on the prestige of the program, according to a 2004 survey (Rostiashvili 2004). The biggest bribes were paid to get into law schools and medical schools. The vast majority of students paid unofficial fees, ranging from $5,000 to $15,000, to tutors to help them "prepare" for university entrance exams. These tutors served on the university's examination committee, which set and graded the entrance exams. Students often paid for these sessions only to secure a passing grade, which they did by including special phrases in their essays that identified them as "tutees" (students' names were not on the tests).

Bribes were so common that people negotiated them right on campus. (One elderly woman reportedly stood at the university's reception area seeking "guidance" from passersby on whom she should approach with the bribe she had prepared to help her grandson gain admission.) The system left students from poor families, especially those in the regions, with little chance of getting a university degree. Even students from middle-class families in Tbilisi had to change their major or choice of university if they could not bribe their way into the school or program they wanted.

By early 2000, public discontent with the system was growing, but nothing changed. The people in power lacked the incentive to alter the status quo, and poorer families, especially those from the regions, had little influence. In 2002, the government adopted a decree called the "Main Directions of Higher Education Development in Georgia," which acknowledged the problems related to corruption and patronage in a system that favored the rich. The decree called for a more transparent entrance examination system, for student vouchers to replace direct grants to institutions, and for proper university accreditation procedures and better management of higher education. The measure failed, because of a lack of support from all levels of government.

Around that time, the number of higher education institutions skyrocketed, rising from 26 public institutions (plus 18 branches) to 235; 209 new licenses for private universities were granted in 2002 alone. The huge number of low-quality institutions accredited in nontransparent ways caused concern among the public, but no one appeared ready to take on the complex task of leading a comprehensive university accreditation system.

Post–2003 Anticorruption Reforms

A new law adopted in 2004 aimed to overhaul the higher education system, including its management, financing, and accreditation processes. Among other things, it called for more transparent entrance exams.

The same year, government officials responded to public demands to force the resignation of the rector of Tbilisi State University over governance issues—a strong signal to academia and the public that the new government was committed to addressing corruption issues. They also demanded resignations from other highly influential elites.

To take full advantage of the government's widespread popularity and the strong political support from high-level officials, the newly appointed minister of education and science, Alexander (Kakha) Lomaia, decided to accelerate the admissions reform process, which had languished under the previous government. Instead of gradually introducing a new entrance exam over a two-year period—in 2006 and 2007, as previously planned—he decided to roll the entire program out at once in 2005. The reforms included four key elements: establishing a single, centralized entrance examination, making it secure and transparent, improving the quality of higher education institutions, and communicating with the public.

Establishing a Single, Centralized Entrance Examination

Following a year and a half of intensive preparations, the first centralized university entrance examinations were administered in July 2005. Exams were offered in three subject areas: Georgian language and literature, math, and foreign languages. A general aptitude test, which examined critical thinking and reasoning skills, was also included, as a way of leveling the playing field for students from less academically challenging schools. Top-scoring entrants were eligible for state scholarships.

Before reform, each university gave its own exams, multiplying the opportunities for corruption. Reformers created a new, independent institution, the National Examination Center, which creates and administers exams for all institutions at 14 centers around Georgia. University professors would no longer be involved in test preparation or grading. Exams were designed to Western standards, using the Baltic countries, Israel, Sweden, the United Kingdom, and the United States as models.

To build public confidence and dispel rumors, the staff of the National Examination Center visited every district in Georgia to consult with stakeholders about the design of the new system and provide information about why particular changes were being made.

Building trust in the new system was not easy. Criticism and skepticism came not just from university staff with stakes in the old way of doing things but from parents and students—even those who stood to benefit from the proposed changes—as well. Escalating the debate, some university administrators accused the government of instituting antinational policies on the grounds that Georgian history was not a mandatory part of the new entrance examinations.

Among the most serious protests was a multiday hunger strike by 180 students. Under the old system, students who successfully completed their studies at a particular college were automatically admitted to the state medical university. Under the new policy, these students had to pass centralized exams to gain admission. Tuition at this college was expensive, and many of its students were sons and daughters of influential members of society. Political pressure over these and other issues grew, leading to fierce debates in Parliament. In the end, the reformers carried the day.

Ensuring a Secure and Transparent Examination System
To eliminate corruption, build public trust, and garner support for the new system, reformers gave security top priority. Entrance exams were printed at the Cambridge University printing house in England. The sealed examinations were sent back to Georgia and delivered in police cars to the vaults of the national bank, where they were stored until test day. Some 700 local proctors, along with 72 Georgian and 20 foreign observers, monitored the exams. International organizations such as Transparency International monitored the entire process. In addition, 470 police officers and 34 doctors were on hand to ensure the security and health of the students.

The monitors were trained to supervise exams and spot cheaters. Tests were identified by barcode rather than student name to help eliminate bias during grading. Closed-circuit television cameras were installed in every testing room, so that parents could monitor the process from a waiting room outside. Completed tests were scanned and made available on a website for added transparency. An appeals procedure was put in place.

Improving the Quality of Institutions of Higher Education
Measures to improve the quality of institutions of higher education have been an important part of the fight against corruption in university

entrance examinations. They have also helped enhance the credibility of the new exams.

Reform included three main approaches. First, in 2005, the Ministry of Education and Science carried out an ambitious institutional accreditation process to eliminate low-quality institutions of higher education, reducing the number of universities from 237 to 43. The new accreditation process evaluated institutions using a set of objective criteria, such as the number of professors, the size of buildings, and the number of books. Although the system was far from perfect, it eliminated the most egregious institutions.

Second, policy makers reformed the financing of higher education, requiring accreditation before an institution could qualify for state funding. At the same time, competition for funding increased, as the government adopted the principle of "the money follows the student" instead of providing grants directly to higher education institutions. Students awarded state scholarships could use them at either public or private institutions.

Third, competition among universities was opened up. Students were allowed to apply to multiple universities in a single year, giving them greater choice. (Before reform, they could apply to only one school a year, making the entire system less competitive.)

Some areas of reform, including accreditation and staff retrenchment, ultimately received only tepid public support, in part because of problems with design and execution. The new higher education accreditation system, for example, guaranteed that institutions fulfilled minimum standards, but it did not guarantee quality. Throughout 2006 and 2007, most instructors at public institutions of higher education had to reapply for their jobs through a competitive process. About 10 percent were not rehired. This loss of jobs by teachers and administrators caused outrage in academia and the media, with critics claiming that the way people were rehired—particularly at Tbilisi State University—was ambiguous, biased, and poorly communicated, both to those affected and to the public.

Communicating with the Public

The government ran an aggressive information campaign, using community meetings, television advertisements, animated commercials, radio announcements and programs, and newspaper inserts to share a set of well-prepared messages. It also produced promotional materials, such as posters, bookmarks, and calendars.

People adversely affected by the reforms also used the media. Some university teachers who had lost their jobs appeared on television and wrote editorials to criticize the reforms and the people behind them. There were many protests outside universities, which included students and teachers. Some opposition leaders used this public dissatisfaction to gain political advantage, but the impact remained limited.

Results

Georgia's once notoriously corrupt university entrance exam has been transformed into a competitive exam based strictly on merit. Wealthy and well-connected students are no longer able to bribe their way into university, and students from the regions now have much greater access to higher education.

Confidence in the Integrity of the New Entrance Examination System

Some 31,000 candidates took the first national entrance examinations, administered July 11–28, 2005. Observers from the International Organization for Fair Elections and Democracy (ISFED), which monitored the 14 testing centers, pronounced the administration of the exams as fair, transparent, and well organized (ISFED 2005). External surveys confirm this view. A 2005 public opinion survey indicated that students, parents, and administrators were satisfied with the new test-taking process (Transparency International 2005). According to the survey, the vast majority of respondents—80 percent of students, 80 percent of parents, and more than 90 percent of administrators—felt confident that the new process was likely to eliminate corruption in university admissions. The vast majority of students and parents also reported understanding the admissions process.

Improved Access to Education by Students from Outside Tbilisi

The new exams increased university access for students from outside the capital, increasing their share of the university population to 61 percent in 2006 (NaEC 2006). Broader access is also reportedly improving student quality. One professor reported having to tear up her syllabus after a few weeks because the new crop of students needed more challenging material.

Stronger Accountability Framework

Reducing corruption in higher education involved strengthening the accountability framework around the exam system (figure 8.1). University insiders can no longer influence admissions, and students can no longer bribe officials to gain admission. Since reform, the only way to enroll in

Figure 8.1   Accountability Framework for University Entrance Examinations

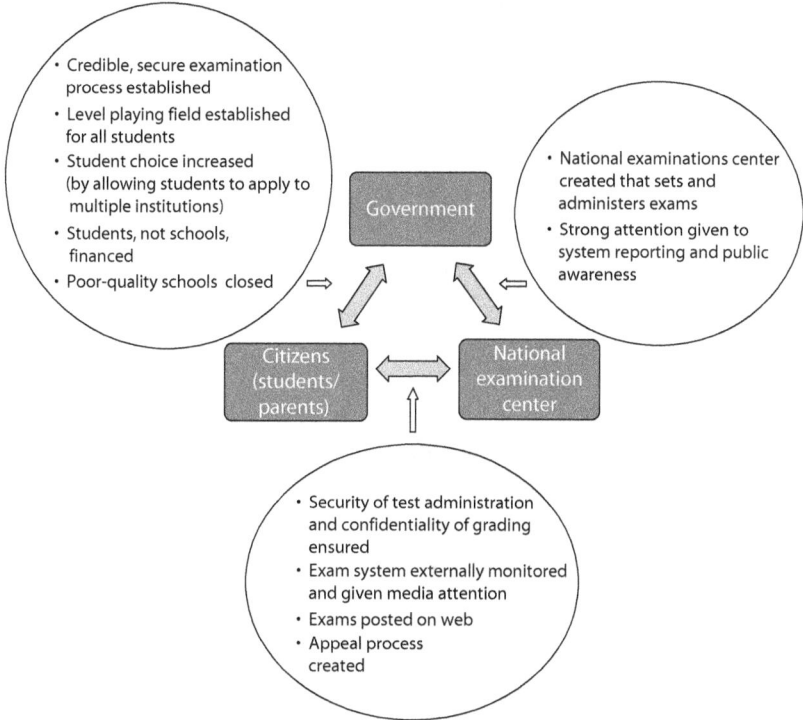

- Credible, secure examination process established
- Level playing field established for all students
- Student choice increased (by allowing students to apply to multiple institutions)
- Students, not schools, financed
- Poor-quality schools closed

Government

- National examinations center created that sets and administers exams
- Strong attention given to system reporting and public awareness

Citizens (students/parents)

National examination center

- Security of test administration and confidentiality of grading ensured
- Exam system externally monitored and given media attention
- Exams posted on web
- Appeal process created

Source: Authors.

university in Georgia has been to pass an exam controlled by an autonomous organization whose officials are not in a position to influence results, thanks to extensive security measures. Making scanned exams publicly accessible and setting up an appeals process for disputing results further ensured a corruption-free environment. Since reform, students have received merit grants directly and been able to apply to multiple schools and programs each year. Parents have benefited, too, by being able to watch exams as they are given and by knowing that all universities meet at least some minimum standards.

Conclusions

The reforms in higher education succeeded for a number of reasons. Strong political will helped establish credibility early by attacking the most egregious symbol of corruption in higher education, the university entrance exam. The design of the exam had been largely completed before the change in government, but its implementation had been slowed by a lack of will and opposition by those who profited from the corrupt status quo. Reformers seized the opportunity created by the change in government to accelerate the introduction of the new exam and begin the reform of the accreditation process, staffing, and financing.

Use of the media to publicize the reforms was also key. The government was able to communicate the reasons for the reform effectively and build widespread public support in the face of stiff opposition by those who stood to lose.

The credibility of the exam was established by the extraordinary measures taken to ensure its integrity, including the use of video cameras and independent observers, the posting of results on the web, and the introduction of an appeals process. The sustainability of these reforms now rests largely on maintaining the new institutions that have been established, largely through executive means, and supporting them through a system of checks and balances to protect them against reform reversal.

CHAPTER 9

Decentralizing Municipal Services

The State of Affairs in 2003

Georgia's municipal infrastructure—water supply, sewerage, solid waste services, local roads—was crumbling in 2003. Local self-governments lacked the resources for capital investment and maintenance.

The pitiful state of Georgia's infrastructure reflects its old age, its overdesigned (and therefore expensive to maintain) technology, inefficient energy use, and lack of routine maintenance. But corruption was also a big part of the problem. Local utility officials sought bribes to connect structures to public water or fix roads. Service quality was so poor that people contracted waterborne diseases. Many services required state subsidies, but leakages in the flow of funds meant that services were perpetually underfunded.

The allocations of targeted subsidies for utilities, particularly water, to consumers were corrupted, and high levels (80 percent) of nonpayments for service were the norm. Local self-governments maintained lists of consumers eligible for social assistance or subsidies for water, but the lists were often falsified, with water officials adding the names of the people who had died or left the country and pocketing the subsidies. Favoritism also prevailed, with targeted subsidies going to relatives and friends of municipal and utility officials. Given the low levels of service provision, weak accountability, and the widely corrupted subsidy system, consumers' willingness to pay for services was extremely low. The tariff collection rate in most cities was 20–30 percent, one of the lowest rates in the world. The problem persisted because legislation failed to provide utilities with the legal clout to disconnect nonpayers from service.

The system of budget allocation to local self-governments was neither clear nor transparent. Negotiations over intergovernmental transfers took place in two stages—first between the Ministry of Finance and the district (*rayon*) authorities and then between *rayon* authorities and local self-governments. Powerful governors and mayors, often of large cities, walked away with much more than their fair share. By retaining significant influence over local self-governments via the negotiated transfer mechanism, the central government effectively obliterated local government autonomy, limiting the scope for citizen voice and oversight over budgeting decisions.

At the same time, according to Vakhtang Lejava, chief adviser to the prime minister, "lack of clear responsibilities and an excessive fragmentation of governments—Georgia was divided into 60 *rayons*, which were in turn divided into 1,110 local self-governments, consisting of towns, settlements, and villages—resulted in diffuse responsibilities and accountabilities, huge public cost to run such a large number of regional and local offices, and abundant opportunities for corruption." Local administrations ran municipalities as fiefdoms of mayors, who were appointed by—and therefore accountable to—the central government. Local budgets were not disclosed to citizens, who were not consulted in the process of identifying priority development projects. Investment projects were often chosen based on the interests of mayors and their friends, and contracts were awarded to a small group of favored contractors.

Post–2003 Anticorruption Reforms

Anticorruption reforms were embedded in the broader reforms of local self-governments and municipal services, which sought to bring government closer to the people by increasing transparency and accountability and strengthening financial discipline in the provision of municipal services. Reforms included three key features.

Clarifying the Legal Framework for Local Self-Governments

In December 2005, a new organic law on local self-governments was adopted. The law consolidated local self-governments into *rayons*. Cities that were directly subordinate to the central government were given the same status as the former *rayons*. As a result of this restructuring, the number of local governments fell from 1,110 to 67, a manageable number for the central government to coordinate with and monitor.

In June 2006, a new Law on Local Budgets was adopted. This law introduced a formula-based equalization grant system and a subnational fiscal database at the Ministry of Finance to monitor budget execution. The two laws strengthened central and local capacity to implement an integrated system of municipal budgeting monitoring and financial reporting.

These reforms laid the foundation for the first municipal elections of mayors, based on the new territorial arrangements, in October 2006. New municipal councils were in place by January 1, 2007, and mayors were elected indirectly by elected council members. Tbilisi's mayor was elected by direct vote in 2010.

The financial management of local self-governments was restructured and made clearer. In 2007, the staff of all local self-governments went through training on the budget preparation process to comply with the Ministry of Finance's instructions for complete changes in financial reporting procedures beginning January 1, 2008. To establish an integrated financial reporting mechanism, all new local self-governments and the Ministry of Finance received computer equipment, software, and tailored technical assistance. These actions enabled the Ministry of Finance to develop, for the first time in 2008, a subnational fiscal analysis database to enhance fiscal oversight and discipline. A direct result of fiscal discipline and oversight actions was the decline in the arrears and defaults on loans of local self-governments, which fell from 23.0 percent in 2002 to less than 0.5 percent in 2011.

The functions of subnational governments were also curtailed, to make them more manageable. Before 2006, subnational governments were the predominant providers of primary education. They also played an important role in health care and social assistance, paying salaries and covering operating costs and facility maintenance. The central government took over functions that had been plagued by corruption. Functions that are now the exclusive responsibility of local governments consist principally of various municipal infrastructure services.

Prosecuting Corrupt Senior Staff and Strengthening Institutions

According to the Ministry of Justice, 165 senior local officials were prosecuted between 2003 and 2010, including 5 governors, 6 mayors,

6 deputy mayors, 93 city council chairs, and 31 deputy city council chairs. This action sent a very strong signal to new staff and raised accountability.

Because of the consolidation of local self-governments, staffing was cut almost in half. Minimum qualifications were prepared, adopted, and enforced. Training increased capacity and changed staffers' mindsets.

To sustain a mechanism to enable local governments to finance needed infrastructure repairs, in 2005, the government began improving the legal, governance, and financial framework of the Georgia Municipal Development Fund, a nonbank financial intermediary that plays an important role in funding municipal infrastructure development. Its supervisory board, chaired by the prime minister, includes representatives of various ministries, Parliament, and nongovernmental organizations. "Its governance structure and human capacity have helped improve municipal services and prevent corruption in the government procurement of goods and services," said Lasha Gotsiridze, the fund's former executive director. At the same time, a capacity-building program for local self-governments was implemented, with the support of various donor agencies, to strengthen the participatory strategic planning processes of all local self-governments, local economic development, financial management, and accounting.

Reforming Municipal Services

To reduce corruption in the targeted water subsidy, in 2006 the government started to consolidate all targeted subsidies to services under a single social assistance program. As part of the overall anticorruption campaign, it improved its targeting and systems of monitoring implementation. As a result, the collection rate rose to 75 percent.

In 2008, the government initiated reforms in the water and wastewater sector. A legal entity of public law—the Water Supply Regional Development Agency—was created under the Ministry of Regional Development and Infrastructure. Urban water and wastewater utilities were consolidated into two state-owned regional companies (LLC Western Water and LLC Eastern Water), which were consolidated into one company at the end of 2009 and merged with the agency at the national level. The United Georgian Water Company is now responsible for sector development and coordination, implementation of sector projects financed by the government or donors, day-to-day operations and maintenance, and interface with customers.

In 2010, in a very bold step, a law was passed to enforce payment for services. The law links payments for all services (water, electricity, gas, telephone, and garbage) to one another and empowers all service utilities to discontinue all service provision if a consumer fails to pay for any service for three consecutive months. Following passage of the law, commercial losses fell from 60 percent in 2004 to 20 percent in 2011.[5]

Results

It is difficult to untangle the anticorruption achievements from the broader reforms of local self-government and municipal service in Georgia. What is clear is the broad array of improvements in governance, especially with respect to local transparency, accountability, and service delivery. Key results are described below.

Improved Municipal Infrastructure, Especially Water Supply

The municipal development sector has improved dramatically since 2003. Public spending to rehabilitate and expand municipal infrastructure increased from $50 million over 1993–2003 to $600 million over 2003–13. Average daily water service increased from 4 hours to 16, the share of rehabilitated municipal roads rose from 10 percent to 75 percent, and the out-of-pocket cost consumers had to pay for service fell by 70 percent. Fraudulent lists of people eligible for targeted subsidies were replaced by an integrated social assistance program. Collection rates for water service increased from 20–30 percent in the early 2000s to 70–75 percent in 2011.

Higher Income of Local Self-Governments

The income of local self-governments rose from about GEL 400 million in 2003 to about GEL 1.7 billion in 2011 (figure 9.1). As a result, according to Minister of Finance Dimitri Gvindadze, municipal service delivery improved. Better intergovernmental fiscal relations and oversight strengthened fiscal discipline, allowing local self-governments' defaults and arrears to the Municipal Development Fund to fall from 22 percent in 2003 to almost zero in 2011.

Development of the Municipal Development Fund

The Municipal Development Fund has grown steadily. It now manages a solid loan portfolio and reinforces fiscal discipline in loan repayment.

Figure 9.1   Local Self-Government Budgets, 2003 and 2011

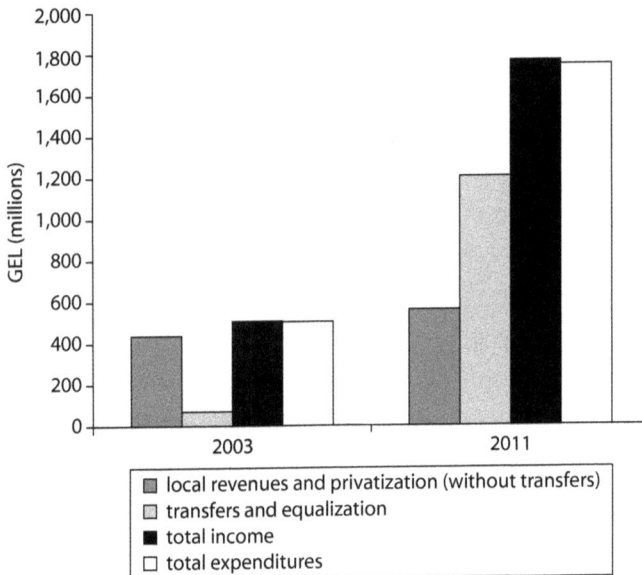

Source: Ministry of Finance data.

It operates as a revolving fund, using its cash flow to fund new projects. From an initial level of GEL 3.9 million in 2001, turnover reached about GEL 230.0 million in 2010, with a portfolio that included five on-lending credits, worth GEL 50.0 million, and 10 grant activities, which funded almost GEL 180.0 million worth of subprojects.

Stronger Accountability Framework

The government launched the reform of municipal and local governments to improve the efficiency of local services and stamp out corruption in their delivery (figure 9.2). As with other sectors, it established credibility by aggressively prosecuting corrupt officials and supporting efforts to improve collections of utility payments, including by disconnecting nonpaying customers.

The size and mandate of local self-governments improved significantly with the establishment of new and focused functions. Election of mayors increased accountability to citizens. The government improved the governance structure of the Municipal Development Fund and made local officials more accountable to their constituents. Local utilities were able to improve their financial situation by increasing collections, which translated into better services for local residents.

Figure 9.2   Accountability Framework for Municipal Service

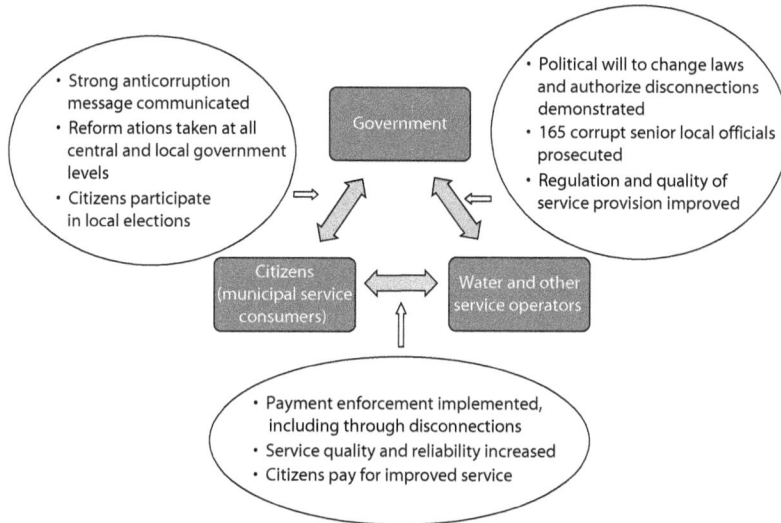

- Strong anticorruption message communicated
- Reform ations taken at all central and local government levels
- Citizens participate in local elections

Government

- Political will to change laws and authorize disconnections demonstrated
- 165 corrupt senior local officials prosecuted
- Regulation and quality of service provision improved

Citizens (municipal service consumers)

Water and other service operators

- Payment enforcement implemented, including through disconnections
- Service quality and reliability increased
- Citizens pay for improved service

Source: Authors.

Conclusions

The government will have to nurture many of the institutional improvements made to local self-governments to sustain them. Some of these challenges go beyond specific anticorruption measures but are nevertheless important to ensure the integrity of municipal and local services and prevent slippages. Key challenges include achieving financial discipline to put municipal services on a cost-recovery basis and create financially sustainable commercial entities, strengthening the human and functional capacities of local self-governments so that they can provide the necessary environment for clean and honest government, and deepening private sector partnerships in service delivery.

CHAPTER 10

Conclusions

Across a range of sectors, the government has tackled corruption in public services that affect the daily lives of Georgians. The design, sequencing, and implementation of reforms varied, but all of the reform initiatives shared certain characteristics that help explain their success.

The 10 Tenets of Success

Ten crosscutting factors, or tenets, seem to account for the success of the reforms in Georgia. Each is discussed below.

1. Exercise Strong Political Will

Strong and sustained political will were essential in the fight against corruption in Georgia. But many countries, including post-revolutionary ones, that started out with political commitment failed to achieve results. What made Georgia different?

Leadership and political commitment came from the top in Georgia. To President Mikheil Saakashvili, it was clear that in 2003 the people had voted to eliminate corruption. "A Georgia without corruption" was a galvanizing slogan for the United Movement in the run-up to the elections and the single dominant theme for the protests leading to the

Rose Revolution, according to Giga Bokeria, who organized many of these protests and is now the head of the National Security Council.

Popular support was key. The fact that more than 90 percent of Georgians supported the new government made it easier to fight corruption aggressively. People were fed up with the petty corruption that had made life miserable. Anticorruption was both a goal and an instrument for modernizing the economy.

2. Establish Credibility Early

Government leaders had a window of opportunity of about eight months for making major changes, according to Vakhtang Lejava, chief adviser to the prime minister. Immediately adopting a zero-tolerance policy for corruption and showing quick and clear results was essential to establishing credibility and keeping the window open long enough for long-term objectives to be met. For former prime minister Lado Gurgenidze, the reforms had to be "fast, binary, simple, and pragmatic and tangibly improve the lives of large numbers of people." Leaders worked to develop a virtuous cycle in which strong political will and clear vision, supported by a flexible strategy, pragmatism, and rapid implementation, led to quick results, which extended the windows of opportunity and reinforced the political will for fighting corruption (figure 10.1).

Figure 10.1   The Virtuous Cycle of Anticorruption Reforms

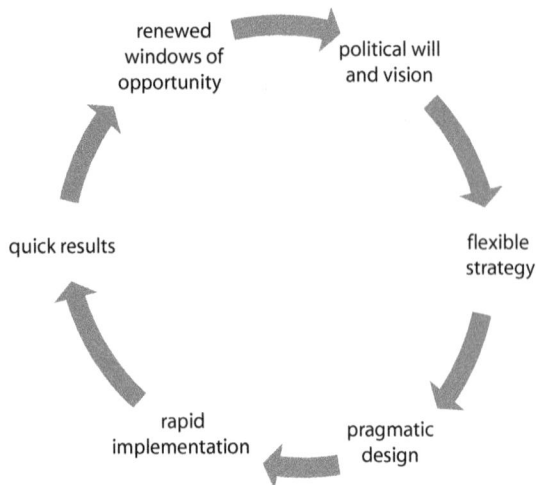

renewed windows of opportunity

political will and vision

flexible strategy

pragmatic design

rapid implementation

quick results

Source: Authors.

Speed of action was critical and fueled a sense of urgency among reformers, for two reasons. First, according to President Saakashvili, "Speed was absolutely critical. Georgia had no more time to lose. It came out in the character of the group—we were impatient, and we still are." Government leaders hardly slept, working 18-hour days to restore the state and provide necessary public services. Second, people were longing for change. Their expectations were enormous. The government was running against time and needed to deliver quickly. Failure to focus on quick results put the reforms—as well as the political careers of the reformers—at risk.

Succeeding, in the words of David Bakradze, speaker of the Parliament, meant that the government had "to destroy the symbols of corruption," foremost among them the thieves-in-law—criminals with close ties to government and immense political power. According to President Saakashvili, "These criminals owed their existence to the state; once the nexus with the state was broken, they became helpless." The government arrested many of the main thieves-in-law early on. It went after corrupt officials and businesspeople who enjoyed unearned privileges under the previous regime.

Another important success factor, according to Minister of Internal Affairs Ivane Merabishvili, was to "show that we are not afraid." New all-glass police offices were a symbol of "openness, transparency, and boldness."

For Levan Bezhashvili, the chairman of the Chamber of Control and former deputy minister of justice in the new government, credibility also meant establishing equality before the law. Many public officials, among them members of Parliament, amassed vast wealth; bringing them to justice sent a strong message that all Georgians were now equal before the law.

Investigating parliamentarians suspected of corruption was difficult under the existing parliamentary rules, so the rules were changed. Before the change, parliamentary approval was needed just to start an investigation—and such approvals were rare. With the rule change, such approval was required only in cases of detention. This seemingly small change represented a breakthrough, as it enabled prosecutors to launch investigations. Once Parliament was faced with a body of evidence, it became impossible—in the face of public opinion—to forestall indictments. The ability of the government to bring parliamentarians to justice—six members of Parliament have been prosecuted since 2003—was the strongest sign at that time that equality before the law had been established and that people with influence were no longer accorded special privileges. Credibility was also enhanced by clarifying the legal basis for fighting corruption and quickly passing a host of anticorruption laws, including anti-mafia legislation, laws permitting the confiscation of illegally obtained property, amendments to the criminal law to permit plea bargaining, and constitutional amendments to rebalance the powers between the different branches of government.

3. Launch a Frontal Assault on Corruption

In many countries promoting reforms, capacity constraints become binding, inducing reformers to settle for piecemeal efforts. What made leaders in Georgia forge ahead with sweeping reforms rather than adopt this approach? Reformers recognized that attacking corruption across many fronts simultaneously was the only way to fight it. They understood that piecemeal reforms would not work, as vested interests would be able to block them. It was essential to adopt a blitzkrieg approach and keep the opposition unbalanced to prevent opponents from resisting them.

Policy makers also understood that many of the reforms were interlinked and that success in one area needed success in others. For the anticorruption reforms in the power sector to succeed, for instance, the state had to improve the availability and reliability of power supply, which required immediate investments in power generation, transmission, and distribution. Public resources were scarce, however. Tax collection needed to improve to fund these investments.

When everything needs fixing, the question is where to begin. Georgia's leaders believed that restoring the rule of law and improving tax collection were necessary first steps. The order of other reforms was driven by the desire to benefit the maximum number of people in the shortest time possible. Not surprisingly, restoring power supply was a priority in 2004, as was deregulating business and ridding higher education of corruption. Some reforms carried inherent risks, as the population would have to share some of the burden for making changes work. Restoring power, for example, required higher power tariffs and more stringent collection. According to Zurab Nogaideli, the former prime minister, government leaders bet that around-the-clock power, a visible and welcome change, would outweigh concerns about higher rates.

4. Attract New Staff

The lack of capable staff often limits the ability to implement reforms. Georgian policy makers overcame human capacity constraints in public institutions by recruiting people from outside, especially people with private sector experience, Western qualifications, or both.

Prime Minister Nika Gilauri's story is revealing. He was working with a power sector consulting company when he received a call from the government asking him to make a presentation to the then prime minister and a few ministers on his solutions for the power sector. After the presentation, he was offered the position of energy minister. Kakha Bendukidze was a prosperous industrialist who had made his fortune in the Russian Federation. He was visiting Georgia and talking to members of the new government on the directions for economic policy when he was offered the job of minister of economic development—a post he immediately accepted.

The infusion of new blood took place not only at the senior levels of government but at all levels. In restaffing the police force, Minister of Internal Affairs Ivane Merabishvili was looking for young, bright, educated, and ethical people who were willing to provide a public service. The primary selection criteria were no previous government experience and a clean past. For Georgia's energy minister in the early days of the new government, Nika Gilauri, the top priority was to "develop a team that would lead the reforms. I invested much of my time in directly recruiting and interviewing people, not only at the deputy minister level but also at the head of department level."

To inspire this new class of public servants and dissuade them from taking bribes, the government needed to pay them a reasonable wage. Doing so proved difficult with limited state revenues. Policy makers therefore adopted unconventional methods. An off-budget fund—financed partly from the Open Society Institute, the United Nations Development Programme, and voluntary contributions by companies and private businesspeople—helped provide performance bonuses to key staff across government agencies. At first, reformers believed that these funds would have to be maintained for several years, until tax collection improved. State revenues, however, increased at a much faster pace than originally expected, allowing the government to close the funds down quickly while still offering competitive salaries and bonuses. The reformers also allowed various public services to charge fees to finance their operations. This change enabled agencies to pay good salaries and reward good work.

To create a new culture of public service, the government took systematic efforts across the board. Probably the most visible success was with the traffic police. Western-style training, new codes of conduct, smart uniforms, and improved equipment gave rise to a new kind of patrol police officer with a strong sense of public service. Police officers—once virtually synonymous with corruption—are now widely believed to be helpful to citizens and are held in high esteem.

5. Limit the Role of the State

Georgia's anticorruption efforts have been based in part on a strong belief in a smaller state, with fewer government regulations and greater economic liberties. Economic problems and the pervasiveness of corruption were viewed as the consequences of the state's intrusion into people's affairs. For former prime minister Lado Gurgenidze, "This was a real experiment in the practical policies of liberty." For Kakha Bendukidze, the former minister of economy, it was clear that "limiting the interface between the citizens and the state was essential to reduce the opportunities for corruption."

Attempts to limit interaction between citizens and the state were made through privatization, business deregulation, and tax reform. For Bendukidze, privatization was essential for restructuring the economy, reining in corruption, and increasing state revenues. Not all reformers shared his belief in privatization. At one meeting, he listed on a white board the public enterprises that could be sold and the revenues their sales might generate. It was only when other ministers saw the potential revenues and thought about how that money might be used that they jumped on board.

Laissez-faire principles were perhaps most visibly on display during the process of business deregulation. Hundreds of licenses, permits, and inspections for various private sector activities were eliminated. At "guillotine"-style meetings chaired by Bendukidze, heads of public agencies would defend their agencies' functions and regulations, describe the value they added, and make the case for why they should be spared. Where a regulation's public good could be identified, reformers looked at the agency's capacity to enforce it. If the agency lacked adequate capacity, the regulations were cut—at least until capacity improved. Entire agencies were eliminated as well, including the agencies responsible for food safety and motor vehicle inspections.

The reformers believed that letting the market work was a solution to many problems. Virtually overnight, for example, utility customers who failed to pay their bills were disconnected. No one—not hospitals or the metro or an influential mining company—was exempt. As a result, collection rates for power supply soared, generating revenues with which to finance much-needed repairs and new investments. The threat of disconnections also dramatically improved the financial condition of the utilities, reducing their dependence on the state. Meanwhile, higher tariffs meant lower consumption, reducing pressure on power supplies. A simplified tax regime with lower rates encouraged tax payments, increasing revenues and new investments.

6. Adopt Unconventional Solutions

Some of the anticorruption reforms—such as negotiating cash payments with jailed corrupt officials and businesspeople in return for their release—were controversial. "The logic was very simple," explains President Saakashvili. "We could not keep every corrupt public official in jail—there were too many. Rather than having them sitting in jail, costing money to a bankrupt state, it was better to take their illegally obtained money and let them go free. Once they paid, they tended to lose steam." In one high-profile case in early 2004, a well-connected businessman was arrested and released after a few days after he paid $14 million. "The amount recovered," notes Saakashvili, "was equivalent to making pension payments for two months, and better than a protracted legal battle." Other extraordinary measures included the use of extrabudgetary funds to top up salaries and the firing of the entire traffic police in one go.

The use of unconventional measures sometimes meant that due process was not followed. Some of the early arrests and treatment of crime bosses, for example, stretched the limits of laws existing at the time. The government moved quickly to revise the criminal code in accordance with international practice, but it cracked down before the legal changes were made. Organizations like Transparency International expressed concern about the weakness and independence of the judicial system and questioned whether the suspects the government rounded up received fair hearings.

Could the government have done things differently? For President Saakashvili and his core group of reformers, the answer is clearly "no." Given the breakdown of the state, they believe, they had to take decisive action, including widespread arrests, quickly; the balance they struck between prosecutorial actions—sometimes viewed as heavy handed—and institutional development was appropriate. Government leaders recognize that given the developments of the past few years, more focus should now be placed on institutions and less on prosecutorial actions. Saakashvili emphasized as much in an address to Parliament in February 2011 in which he called for a "shift from prosecutions to a public service culture."

7. Develop a Unity of Purpose and Coordinate Closely

Given the holistic nature of the anticorruption reforms, unity of purpose and close coordination among key reformers was essential. How was that achieved, given the rapid pace of change?

Several factors contributed. First, the core team of policy makers was small, shared values regarding the direction of public policy, and stayed together. Second, there was intensive coordination at the level of the cabinet of ministers. The cabinet met frequently; policies were debated, often hotly; and decisions were made. Third, several high-level commissions were established to guide reforms in different areas, such as transport, taxes, energy, and privatization. Anticorruption was often seen as an inseparable component of the sectoral reforms to be undertaken. Fourth, as needed, ad hoc meetings were held on key issues. The sense of urgency that prevailed fostered very close coordination.

Although much of the decision making was made at the level of the cabinet, the president set the overall agenda and priorities and was engaged in key decisions. The parliamentary leadership was also closely involved, as many of the debates took place in Parliament. For Speaker David Bakradze, "anticorruption was a winning argument" in Parliament and helped secure support for the reforms.

8. Tailor International Experience to Local Conditions

Many countries have faced the challenges Georgia faced. Georgian policy makers learned from their experience. Plea bargaining, for example—which was key to early prosecutions, particularly in high-profile cases where testimony from subordinates often sealed the fate of corrupt higher-level officials—was adopted from the U.S. judicial system. Anti-mafia legislation was modeled on legislation in Italy and the United States. And much of Georgia's police training was based on practices in the United States and Europe. It was fortuitous that many members of the new government had been educated abroad and seen first-hand how things could be done differently. Policy makers learned not only from success stories but also from the failures of economic and anticorruption reforms in many countries of the former Soviet Union.

Reformers drew on international experience. But, they are quick to point out, they adapted it to Georgia's unique circumstance and developed their own solutions.

9. Harness Technology

Technology, some of it home grown, was a key component of the anticorruption effort. Its adoption eliminated many direct contacts between public officials with citizens, reducing opportunities for bribery. Technology also helped streamline public services, made them easier to monitor, and simplified transactions for citizens.

The issuance of passports is a case in point. Before reform, getting a passport was riddled with delays and informal payments. Today, citizens submit the necessary documents, pay the fees (which are differentiated based on whether regular or urgent processing is requested), and receive a text message on their cell phone when their passport is ready for pick-up. Regular service takes just 10 days; expedited service takes 24 hours. Georgian citizens living overseas can apply for passports online, verifying their identity via a Skype call with public registry officials. Other examples of the use of technology abound, from the paperless office in the police department to the electronic database for land registration to the recent expansion of e-filing for income taxes, which accounted for almost 80 percent of returns in 2010.

10. Use Communications Strategically

President Saakashvili had excellent political instincts and kept a finger on the pulse of the population, according to former prime minister Zurab Nogaideli. These instincts were important for decisions on key reforms. The increases in the power tariff, for example, were made possible because of the clear sense by the leadership that the political cost of higher tariffs was lower than the political cost of lack of power. Saakashvili valued his close contacts with the people, prompting him to travel frequently around the country. The government as a whole made efforts to gather genuine feedback from the population, often with the help of reputable foreign public relations and opinion research companies, and then adjust its reform interventions to reflect public sentiments.

Early on, government leaders used the media effectively to share images of high-profile arrests of corrupt officials. Even tax evaders were arrested with cameras rolling. Using media in this way spread the word that corruption was no longer tolerated, changing people's views about what was acceptable. "Attacking the symbols of corruption and showing results was key to changing the mindset of the population," says Gigi Ugalava, the mayor of Tbilisi. "Institutional change by itself may not have been enough. This change in mindset is the Georgian transformation."

Reforms themselves, however, were not well communicated initially, contributing to feelings of ill will toward government—most prominently displayed during street protests in 2007 and 2009. Following the protests, government leaders revisited their communications strategy. They introduced town hall meetings across the country in which senior policy makers and ministry officials showcased their programs and results. Beginning in 2009, public discussions of reform challenges and opportunities in various sectors—health, municipal services, tax administration, and business environment—were held. The first private sector roundtable with Georgian businesspeople on tax issues was held in the spring of 2011.

To stay in touch with sentiment on the street, the government conducted formal polling and interacted informally with the public. These polls provide insight into citizens' concerns as well as their views on the impact of reforms.

What Are the Remaining Challenges for Georgia?

Georgia's transformation since 2003 has been remarkable. The lights are on, the streets are safe, and public services are corruption free. A key driver of these changes, which comes through clearly from the case studies, has been the robust use of executive power. Georgia's strong executive branch was able to change incentives, eliminate many corrupt institutions, and build new public institutions. It also prosecuted criminals, officials, and businesspeople on charges of tax evasion, corruption, and criminality. In any anticorruption strategy, both elements—institutional development and prosecutorial actions—are essential.

Did Georgia get the balance right? The emphasis early on was on prosecution (figure 10.2). Many decision makers in government viewed these actions as essential to restoring trust in the state and establishing the credible threat of punishment for corruption.

Figure 10.2   The Right Balance between Prosecutorial Action and Institution Building in Fighting Corruption?

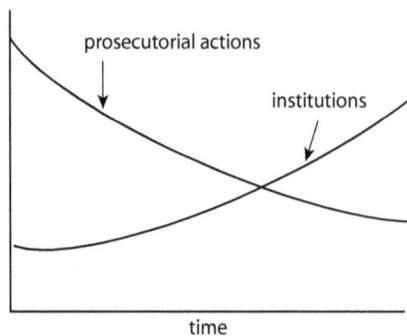

Source: Authors.

Institutions for public service have taken longer to develop and evolve with the needs of society, but active state management has helped create many new institutions for public service. According to Giga Bokeria, the head of the National Security Council, challenges ahead include strengthening institutions and human resources to establish a functional, professional, and highly qualified bureaucracy. Recent government statements and actions suggest that such a shift is under way.

But the role of a strong executive still remains the single biggest driver of change. Indeed, much of the success of the anticorruption reforms can be attributed to the small, committed team in the executive branch, which draws its considerable power from the president and which oversees the day-to-day functioning of government. Some observers are concerned about this concentration of power. As Transparency International (2011, 15) notes in its National Integrity System Assessment for Georgia, ". . . the concentration of power at the top tier of the executive branch and the weak system of checks and balances creates possibilities for abuse and raises concerns about the commitment to the rule of law."

How can the system of checks and balances be strengthened? The public institutions responsible for oversight of the executive branch are Parliament, the judiciary, the public defender, and the Chamber of Control, the supreme public audit agency. According to Transparency International, the legal framework governing these agencies and other aspects of oversight is largely in place and constantly being strengthened. The Council of Europe noted that the constitutional amendments adopted by Parliament on October 15, 2010, "better guarantee the independence of the judiciary, substantially strengthen the role and powers of the parliament and provide for a better and more comprehensive system of checks and balances between the different branches of power" (PACE 2011, 2). The amended law on conflict of interests is rigorous, requiring, among other things, public disclosure of assets of public officials.

The ruling party has a large majority in Parliament and in local elected bodies. The legislative leadership is closely aligned with the executive branch. Vigorous debates on government policy take place, but the lack of a strong opposition limits closer scrutiny of the executive branch by Parliament. The development of an effective opposition is an evolutionary process in a new democracy, though some argue that the lack of equal access to financing and the media make it hard for such an opposition to emerge (Transparency International Georgia 2011).

Strengthening the system's checks and balances requires further development of the judiciary (Freedom House 2010). Much has been achieved in modernizing the judiciary, but more needs to be done. Most judges are young and inexperienced, and they are often overshadowed by a well-resourced and powerful prosecutor's office.[5] The lack of lifetime appointments and the threat of relocation to remote jurisdictions make it difficult for judges to act independently. Accordingly, the judiciary remains among the least-respected institutions in Georgia (Caucasus Research Resource Centers 2010). The government recognizes the concerns about the judiciary and points to its continued efforts to strengthen it, including by introducing jury trials for criminal cases in 2012 and lifetime appointments for judges starting in 2013.

For its part, the public defender's office is becoming a credible institution (Transparency International Georgia 2011). Though it has no power of enforcement and can make recommendations for changes or action only in cases of human rights violation, it serves an important function in the overall system of checks and balances.

As for strengthening external public oversight, capacity constraints limit the effectiveness of the oversight function of the Chamber of Control. A modernization program, supported by donors, is helping ease this constraint. Changes in legislation governing the chamber (passed in 2009) and an increase in staff capacity to carry out modern audits (achieved through intensive training and twinning arrangements with established supreme audit agencies in Europe) are promising steps.

Another key institution in most countries is the media. Georgia's media is still in a nascent stage of development in monitoring the results of anticorruption efforts and exposing corruption in public services. It played a very constructive role in the early fight against corruption, but there is concern that it is no longer capable of serving as a watchdog. Many nonprofit organizations (including Freedom House, IREX, and the Bertelsmann Stiftung) have argued that the media lacks the independence and capacity to report objectively on stories involving the state (Transparency International Georgia 2011). The legal framework is robust in protecting media freedom. The concern is more about the ownership structure of major media outlets, which is opaque. Critics argue that the owners of media outlets are close allies and associates of the leadership and reluctant to report objectively on stories of state interest.

Increasing citizen voice in public policy formulation and implementation is also a work in progress. Input from citizens needs to be a vital part of the development and implementation of public policies and sectoral anticorruption strategies. It can be particularly helpful in monitoring progress toward target outcomes and exposing cases of corruption. Several steps have already been taken in this direction. Civil society organizations are members of the Interagency Coordinating Council for Combating Corruption, established in December 2008, which crafted a new anticorruption strategy and action plan. The appointment of a business ombudsman to facilitate dialogue between government and business, particularly on taxes, is another step toward giving citizens greater voice. More initiatives are needed to help build the capacity of civil society organizations.

Are Georgia's Anticorruption Reforms Replicable Elsewhere?

Georgia's anticorruption reforms followed a revolution that had overwhelming popular support. For this reason, some observers believe that they are the product of a unique historical turning point, making them difficult to replicate elsewhere.

Every country has its own set of institutions and political economy and must find its own path to fighting corruption. But much of Georgia's reform story is indeed replicable. There is nothing specific to Georgia in the 10 tenets discussed above—in some ways, they are home truths. Many countries have deregulated businesses and opened up the economic space for private entrepreneurship or established a fair and transparent university entrance system, or ensured power supply reliability. And they have done so without first going through a revolution.

Many of the ways in which Georgia implemented reform—including the development of a virtuous cycle of reforms that built early credibility for the government—are replicable. Reform of the public and civil registries relied largely on technical innovation; other countries could follow similar paths. The importance of changing the mindset—and the role of the leadership in doing so—is also a transferable notion. As for Georgia's multifront assault on corruption, no country has successfully dealt with systemic corruption with piecemeal reforms, suggesting that only a comprehensive approach may be viable. Harnessing the media to expose corruption and using communication to garner popular support for fighting it are also strategies that other countries can adopt.

Most important is the notion that public services can be cleaned up. Many developing countries are struggling to improve their public services and free their citizens from the burden of bribes. Georgia's extraordinary experience provides hope and some ideas for how they can do so.

In Summary

Since 2003, Georgia has had unique success in fighting corruption in public services. Many countries in the world are struggling with the same problem. Georgia has proven that success can be achieved in a relatively short period of time given strong political will and concerted action by the government. By no means is this fight over—much remains to be done, especially with respect to strengthening institutions (the best safeguard against a relapse of corruption) and ensuring an adequate system of checks and balances. Although every country has a unique set of initial conditions and the nature of the corruption problem and the type of political economy differ, many elements of Georgia's story can be replicated in other countries. Georgia's success destroys the myth that corruption is cultural and gives hope to reformers everywhere who aspire to clean up their public services.

Notes

1. Prosecutions were not limited to people in charge of collections. The head of the wholesale energy market was prosecuted and jailed for corruption, as was the minister of energy.
2. In 2005, Parliament adopted a power sector strategy that was the basis for long-term sector reforms. A key element of the strategy addresses energy security and import dependency of the power supply.
3. Concerned that employees on their way out might seek revenge, Egiashvili hired security guards to watch over the paper-based archive of technical inventory. Fortunately, fired staff left without incident.
4. Data suggest that when the state has an interest in the outcome of a case, it prevails: in 2009, for example, just 18 of 18,392 prosecutions resulted in acquittals (Transparency International Georgia 2011).
5. Data provided by the United Georgian Water Company.

References

24 Saati (24 Hours) *Newspaper*. 2006. May 10, Tbilisi.

Alenova, Olga. 2010. "We Are Not Police—We Are Human Beings." *Kommersant Vlast* 12 (866), March 29. http://www.kommersant.ru/doc/1341809.

BCG Research. 2006. http://www.bcg.ge.

Caucasus Research Resource Centers. 2010. *Caucasus Barometer Survey*. Tbilisi: Caucasus Research Resource Centers.

Civil.ge. 2002. "Human Rights Watch Protests Interior Minister's Initiative." November 26. http://www.civil.ge/eng/article.php?id=2781.

The Economist. 2010. "Georgia's Mental Revolution." August 19.

Forbes. 2009. "Tax Misery and Reform Index." *Forbes*, New York. http://www.forbes.com/global/2008/0407/060_2.html.

Freedom House. 2010. *Nations in Transition 2010*. New York: Freedom House.

Georgian Young Lawyers' Association. 2005. http://gyla.ge.

GORBI (Georgia Opinion Research Bureau International). 2000. *Corruption Survey, 2000 Report*. Tbilisi: GORBI.

———. 2011. *Crime and Security Survey, Georgia*. Tbilisi: GORBI.

Gurgenidze, Lado. 2009. "Georgia's Search for Economic Liberty: A Blueprint for Reform in Developing Economies." *Development Policy Outlook* 2 (June): 5–8, American Enterprise Institute for Public Policy Research, Washington, DC.

IRI (International Republican Institute). 2010. Washington, DC.

ISFED (International Society for Fair Elections and Democracy). 2005. *Annual Report*. Tbilisi: ISFED.

Karosanidze, Tamuna, and Camrin Christensen. 2005. *Stealing the Future: Corruption in the Classroom*. Tbilisi: Transparency International Georgia.

Ministry of Finance. 2011. Data. Tbilisi.

Ministry of Justice. 2011. *Seven Years That Changed Georgia*. Tbilisi: Ministry of Justice.

NaEC (National Educational Commission). 2006. *Report on Unified Entrance Examinations*. Tbilisi: NaEC.

National Bank of Georgia. 2002. *Annual Report*. Tbilisi: National Bank of Georgia.

————. 2003. *Annual Report*. Tbilisi: National Bank of Georgia.

PACE (Parliamentary Assembly of the Council of Europe). 2011. *The Honoring of Obligations and Commitments by Georgia*. Document 12554, March 28. PACE, Strasbourg, France.

Rostiashvili, Ketevan. 2004. *Corruption in the Higher Education System of Georgia*. Tbilisi: Transnational Crime and Corruption Center, Georgia Office.

State Department for Statistics of Georgia. 2003. *Statistical Yearbook of Georgia*. Tbilisi: State Department for Statistics of Georgia.

Transparency International. 2005. *Stealing the Future. Corruption in the Classroom*. Tbilisi: Transparency International.

————. Various years. *Global Corruption Barometer*. Tbilisi: Transparency International.

————. 2011. "Georgia: National Integrity System Assessment." Tbilisi: Transparency International.

World Bank. 2004. *World Development Report: Making Services Work for Poor People*. Washington, DC: World Bank.

————. 2010a. "Georgia Trade Brief." In *World Trade Indicators 2009/10*. Washington, DC: World Bank. http://www.worldbank.org/wti.

————. 2010b. *BEEPS at-a-Glance: Business Environment and Enterprise Performance*. Washington, DC: World Bank.

————. Various years. *Doing Business*. Washington, DC: World Bank. http://www.doingbusiness.org.

World Bank, and EBRD (European Bank for Reconstruction and Development). 2011. *Life in Transition Survey 2*. Washington, DC, and London: World Bank, and EBRD.

WTO (World Trade Organization). 2010. *Trade Policy Review*. WT/TPR/S/224/Rev., January 19.

www.ingramcontent.com/pod-product-compliance
Lightning Source LLC
Chambersburg PA
CBHW071053280326
41928CB00050B/2494